# SYMBOL & ICON

# SYMBOL & ICON

*Dionysius the Areopagite
and the Iconoclastic Crisis*

Filip Ivanovic

PICKWICK *Publications* · Eugene, Oregon

SYMBOL AND ICON
Dionysius the Areopagite and the Iconoclastic Crisis

Pickwick Publications
An imprint of Wipf and Stock Publishers
199 W. 8th Ave., Suite 3
Eugene, OR 97401

www.wipfandstock.com

ISBN13: 978-1-60899-335-2

*Cataloging-in-Publication data:*

Ivanovic, Filip.

Symbol and icon : Dionysius the Areopagite and the iconoclastic crisis / Filip Ivanovic.

xii + 104 p. ; 23 cm. — Includes bibliographical references and index.

ISBN13: 978-1-60899-335-2

1. Pseudo-Dionysius, the Areopagite. 2. Iconoclasm. I. Title.

BR65.D66 I85 2010

Manufactured in the U.S.A.

*To the loving memory of my great-uncle,*
*Branko Djurisic (1932–1996),*
*whose unselfish interest in my upbringing and education*
*I will never forget*

Ἀληθῶς ἐμφανεῖς εἰκόνες εἰσι τὰ ὁρατὰ τῶν ἀοράτων
(Dionysius Areopagita *Epistola* X)

# Contents

# Preface

The book that stands before the reader is the result of my several years long studies of Byzantine philosophical and theological tradition. At the beginning of my interest in philosophy, I read the famous Basil Tatakis's book *Byzantine Philosophy*, a milestone work in the history of eastern philosophical tradition. Since then, Byzantine intellectual history has become the focus of my academic work.

Exploring Byzantine thought was, and it still is, like a quest for a hidden treasure, a wandering through a labyrinth that leads to an unimaginable richness of human intellectual activity. There I found metaphysics, ethics, aesthetics, rhetoric—all expressed in allegorical, mystical forms, full of concealed meanings and secret pathways. In one word, I found there everything that fascinated me and inclined me to study philosophy. In this journey, I became particularly fond of early periods of Byzantine tradition, and my attention was especially captured by Maximus the Confessor and Dionysius the Areopagite, maybe the most "mystical" Christian thinkers.

The notions that mark the Areopagite's thought—namely, hierarchy, light, apophatic and cataphatic theologies, and the divine darkness—as well as his special attention to symbols, inspired me to deepen my knowledge of his writings. The iconoclastic controversy, on the other hand, was known to me only from a few historical accounts; my familiarity with the doctrinal features of the dispute was somewhat vague. However, my practical every-day experience with the Orthodox reverence for icons and their high significance for the Orthodox faith, made me recognize some important features of the icon during my study of the Dionysian writings. Then I started to collect more information on Byzantine aesthetics, theology of the icon, and especially the "theoretical" aspect of the iconoclastic crisis, in order to explore the formation of the iconological doctrines in the writings of the defenders of images. I was surprised that all the studies I read only superficially mention Dionysius' influence on the "icon issue." That inspired me to try to examine this influence and point out the significance of the Areopagite's thought for the iconophile theology, especially since this forms an inseparable part of the living tradition of Orthodox Christianity, and this book represents a result of this effort. Whether I succeeded in my intention, will be the reader's judgment. My intention was not to present my work as final or extraordinary, but just to point to an aspect of icon theology that deserves more attention.

Here I would like to thank the editors and staff of Pickwick Publications at Wipf and Stock Publishers who showed their confidence in me and made it possible for me to publish my first academic book in my field of interest. This is also my first book in English, which makes my satisfaction and my gratitude to them even greater.

I feel obliged to express my deepest thanks to my professors from the University of Bologna, Prof. Dino Buzzetti (Department of Philosophy) and Prof. Enrico Morini (Department of Paleography and Medieval Studies), who served as my supervisors during my undergraduate and postgraduate studies in philosophy. They gave me full support in the development of my academic interests and helped in improving my research skills. They will always be good models of friends and teachers.

I would also like to thank my close friends, especially those coming from professions other than mine, who never stop to being curious and who constantly show their interest in my work, despite its "unpopularity," vagueness, and often incomprehensibility.

In the end, the greatest gratitude goes to my family, without whose unselfish support and loving care I would not have been able to realize my personal and professional endeavors.

# Abbreviations

CH      *Corpus hermeticum: con testo greco, latino e copto.* Edited with commentary by A. D. Nock, A.-J. Festugière, and Ilaria Ramelli. Bompiani il pensiero occidentale. Milano: Bompiani, 2005

CSHB      *Corpus Scriptorum Historiae Byzantinae,* edited by B. G. Nieburhii, Bonnae: Impensis Ed. Weberi, 1839, 2 vols.

Mansi      *Sacrorum Conciliorum nova et amplissima collectio,* edited by J. D. Mansi, Florence, 1759 (1960)

Oratio      *Orationes Tres adversus eos qui Sacras Imagines Abjiciunt,* Iohannes Damascenus. Columns 1227–1421 in PG 94

PG      Patrologiae cursus completus: Series graeca. Edited by J.-P. Migne. 162 vols. Paris, 1857–1886

PL      Patrologiae cursus completus: Series latina. Edited by J.-P. Migne. 217 vols. Paris, 1844–1864

# Introduction

## STARTING POINT

In the symbolic dimension of Christian tradition, the concept of image undoubtedly occupies a central place. In the everyday life of a contemporary Christian icons are an integrating, but also indispensable, part of the cult, whose orthodoxy is never put in question.

However, the history of icons is all but calm. As usually happens in human history, no phenomenon of a certain importance can be affirmed and confirmed without being compromised. In the same way, the path of the icon has been marked by profound discords and even stained with blood. As a matter of fact, an apparently simple question provoked disputes, civil wars, and both political and intellectual confrontations. The concept of the icon defied the Christian understanding of art and beauty, and challenged the very sense of the faith and liturgy. On a deeper level icons posit the difficult-to-resolve problem of "big questions," expressed in dualisms—sensible and intelligible, visible and invisible, matter and spirit. Furthermore, the question arises on the possibility of circumscription of the Divine, which is, by rule, unrepresentable, incomprehensible, and ineffable. In another context, the life of the icon in Byzantium also represented an important sign of historical circumstances and political events.

The subject of iconography started one of the longest (ca. 120 years) and most violent theological disputes within the Byzantine Empire and Orthodox Church—the iconoclastic controversy, whose historical development we will examine in one of the forthcoming chapters.

Since the cult of images signed the entire cultural history of the humankind, an exhaustive discussion of this theme should find its starting point already in times of classical antiquity, and our question should be concentrated on the concept of sacred image, i.e., on the representation of the divine. It is, at first sight, a simple question, which, however, does not offer uniform answers. Even so, the diversity of opinions on sacred icons in the ancient period does not incite surprise, if one bears in mind the variety of beliefs and religious practices of the Greco-Roman world, especially taking into consideration its millenary existence and extremely vast territorial extension, from Spain and Ireland to India and Persia. From this perspective, it is not difficult to understand that in ancient times, the comprehension of sacred image was labelled by dissonant voices. It is not possible to further elaborate on the ancient concept of image here, since this book is concentrated on the specific Christian dimension of the problem. However, in an exemplary line, we could trace two ancient visions of the image of god.

On the one hand, image (*eidolon*) had a crucial position in the ancient world—in certain contexts, *eidolon* was a synonym for *psyche*, which designated the human soul after death of the body. In this sense, *eidolon* lacks of matter; it is completely articulated in form, and since it is a visible form, it represents an exact replica of the dead person. On the other hand, image for Plato, as one could suppose, is doubtful or false, since for him every image of an object, (e.g., a table or a bed), is insufficient or false. This vision of image will continue to exist in the thought of Porphyry, Iamblichus, Proclus, and others.[1] However, it is important to notice here that the ancient philosophical-theological background of the representation of the divine is quite different from the Christian point of view. For ancient Greeks, it was not God who created the world, but the world gave birth to gods. So gods proceed, generate, and proliferate in what we might call causal-genetic rows, in which one divinity gives birth to another and so on. Between men and gods there is an insurmountable difference—the gift of immortality that gods posses and the mortality of all humans. However, in Pindarus' words, "From one mother we both draw our breath." Probably herein lies the reason for the different attitudes towards the images of the divine in the ancient times—since both humans and gods were birthed by the earth, gods are not uncreated. Therefore, the attribute of being impossible to be circumscribed cannot

1. On the historical-linguistic evolution of idols and icons, see Saïd, "Images grecques," 11–20.

be applied to them, as in the case of the Christian God. That is why the art was public, the artists made representations of gods in agreement with the public, and there were no prohibitions on creating the sacred images. This went so far that the gods were not really distinguished from their representations, and it is not a surprise that Hegel called the artist a theologian of Greek religion.

Although Christianity absorbed many ancient traditions, especially the Greek, whose influence cannot be disregarded, the main source of every Christian discourse is naturally the Sacred Scripture. In this sense, the solution of every Christian problem, especially in the first centuries, would have to be looked for in the Bible. Therefore, the disputes on images also found their source in the Bible, in the second commandment, in Deuteronomy, etc. Perhaps because of these prohibitions we do not have any proof regarding the veneration of icons before the third century. The only examples of the discussion on Christian representations in the literature of this period are some critical notes of Tertullian on the images of the Good Shepherd on chalices, and the list of symbolic objects adequate for being represented on seals, made by Clement of Alexandria.[2] When, in the fourth century, Christian art became the object of more particular comments, these were in the beginning hostile and restrictive.[3] However, no systematic defense or confutation of images can be found before the famous iconoclastic controversy, which had its beginning in the eighth century.

During the controversy, the two opposed parties, iconoclasts and iconophiles (or iconodules), developed their arguments for and against icons. It is interesting to note that the iconoclastic party was led mainly by emperors and supporters of the imperial policy, while the fraction of the defenders of icons was composed of monks, bishops and theologians—a fact that does not surprise much if one bears in mind that the iconoclastic crisis actually broke out with the order of Leo III to remove the icon of Christ from the Gate of Chalke.

Both parties claimed to have enough arguments to defend their positions. As was usual in the epoch, the contents of these arguments were not only the fruit of individual and independent intellectual capacities, but

2. Koch, *Die altchristliche Bilderfage*, 9–10 and 14ff.

3. The Council of Elvira; the letter of Eusebius to the empress Constantia (Koch, *Die altchristliche Bilderfage*, 42).

their authors appealed to authorities, which mainly were the Scripture and texts written by the Fathers of the Church. It was an indispensable practice without which the argumentative discourse would have lost its force. A particular interest for the discourse on icons provokes an authoritative person, whose authority came only after the Bible—Pseudo-Dionysius the Areopagite. During the Middle Ages, Dionysius was considered an incontestable master and a theologian of the greatest importance. The contents of his writings would lead one to think that it would have been inevitable for the disputed parties to invoke his authority in order to justify their own positions.

THE AIM

The purpose of this work will be to examine what contribution the writings of the Areopagite could have provided the theology of icons and in what measure they were actually used during the iconoclastic controversy. An ulterior stimulus to engage in the work in this sphere consists of two points: firstly, Dionysius the Areopagite was effectively used and invoked during the iconoclastic controversy, and secondly, both the Areopagite and the protagonists of the crisis profoundly marked the history of Christianity and, therefore, the history of contemporary civilization. It follows that the relationship between Dionysius and the dispute on images merits being the theme of an exhaustive and detailed study, which naturally does not pretend to be final.

The study encompasses four parts. Chapters 1 and 2 could be regarded as introductory, since there I describe the main points of Dionysius' thought and expose the principal features of the historical-doctrinal development of the iconoclastic controversy. In the third chapter I examine the Areopagite's thought on symbols and the place that these have in his system. Chapter 4 is intended to represent a synthesis of Dionysius' notions and the crucial doctrinal elements that were employed by the defenders of icons.

In the first chapter, I examine in general terms the thought of Dionysius the Areopagite with specific regards to his place within the context of Christian literature. I start with the unavoidable discussion concerning the true identity of Dionysius, and offer some of the hypotheses that tried to identify him with this or that author of the late antique period.

The main controversy in the scholarship that deals with the Areopagite is whether he was truly a Christian writer, or "just" a Neo-Platonist whose interest was to include Neo-Platonic elements in the Christian doctrine. I am inclined to agree that Dionysius was genuinely Christian, and it is in this sense that my comparison of his thought with the main lines of Neo-Platonic philosophy should be understood. I then proceed with describing the Areopagite's notions of apophatic and cataphatic theologies and his exposition of the characteristics of the divinity. Finally, I give an analysis of the role of celestial and ecclesiastical hierarchies, their laws and purpose, together with one of Dionysius' main preoccupations, the deification of man, i.e., the ascent of the soul to God.

The second chapter is dedicated to the description of the iconoclastic controversy. Firstly, I give a brief account of the historical events that marked the course of the controversy. Secondly, I posit the question concerning the causes that might have provoked the negative attitude towards icons, and their socio-political and theological backgrounds.

Chapter 3 deals with the symbolic theory of Dionysius, which could also represent his opinion on images. What are symbols and what is their role according to the Areopagite? This is the question that this chapter tries to answer.

Finally, Chapter 4 is focused on the comparative exposition of the theology of icon and Dionysian thought. This is also where I describe some types of icons and the arising of their cult before the era of iconoclasm. This part examines the writings of John of Damascus, Theodore the Studite, and, to some extent, Patriarch Nicephorus, and shows the explicit or implicit influences that Dionysius exerted on them. I then give the definition of the Council of Nicaea, which restored the veneration of icons, and identify the fragments in which the Dionysian influence can be seen. In the end, I discuss the relationship between the apophatic theology, and the main notions in the Areopagite's thought, and icons, emphasizing the importance that this connection maintained during the course of Byzantine-Orthodox spirituality.

## THE MATERIAL

The material used in this study is divided into two groups. The first group, the primary sources, could also be divided into two parts: the writings of Dionysius the Areopagite, and the works written by theologians who participated in the iconoclastic dispute, together with the decisions of the Council of Nicaea. The second group represents the secondary literature, and consists of monographs and studies that in various ways deal with Dionysius the Areopagite, his doctrine and theological system, different aspects of the iconoclastic controversy and its protagonists, and the general issues of the theology of icons and their veneration.

The literature on icon is vast and rich and the history of images has been told from diverse angles: historical, literary, philosophical, theological, and artistic. Many texts have been dedicated to the Byzantine iconoclastic controversy, and much has been written on the orthodox theology of icon. However, what lacks are the works that concentrate on the specific theme of the influence that Fathers of the Church, especially Dionysius, exerted on the thought of famous defenders of icons. One of the most important works in this sphere is a long essay of Gerhart B. Ladner, which, unfortunately, does not analyze in detail the relationship between iconoclasm and Dionysius, but concentrates on other Fathers.[4] Further, Ernst Kitzinger, in his classical article, gave many clarifications on the cult of images before the controversy, but he too dedicates little space to the writings of the Areopagite.[5] Almost all the works that deal with the iconoclastic crisis and with the doctrine of icons mention and briefly discuss the work of Dionysius, but none has examined this relationship in detail.[6]

Exception in this field of modern scholarship are two works by Andrew Louth, which however, in my opinion, deserve to be further developed and completed.[7]

## THE METHOD

The method employed in this study is historical-comparative, since it is the most suitable for the analysis of philosophical and theological systems

4. Ladner, "The Concept of the Image," 1–34.

5. Kitzinger, "The Cult of Images," 83–150.

6. A considerable space is given to Dionysius' influence on the formation of Byzantine aesthetics in Bychkov, *L'estetica bizantina*.

7. Louth, "St. Denys the Areopagite," 329–39; Andrew Louth, "Truly Visible Things," 15–24.

that belong to different temporal settings. The focus will be on original texts of Dionysius and protagonists of the iconoclastic controversy, and on the identification of points of convergence, which will lead to a comparison between doctrines with a synoptic-synthetic view of their features. The method will, therefore, be *systematic*, since the research will focus on understanding and exposing various connections and relationships, but also *hermeneutical* because it will offer the interpretation of the mentioned texts. The hermeneutical method in a systematic theological lens will serve as the main method to develop this analysis.

It is important here to note that, when dealing with original texts, it is of utmost significance to respect the internal integrity of the texts, which are written by a specific person in a specific spatio-temporal settlement. This is why I tried to provide ample textual citations, so that reader could engage in his own interpretations and understandings of the thought that I seek to examine and connect.

Since this book deals with a problem that might be attributed a multidisciplinary character, my effort was to view it from different angles. This sense could also apply to my bibliographic choices, which refer to studies written by philosophers, theologians, historians of art, Byzantinists, and others. All these disciplines contributed to providing diverse contextual perspectives, which can provide a broader and fuller view of the phenomena in question.

## SOME PRELIMINARY REMARKS

As we will see in the first chapter, the identity of Dionysius the Areopagite is still unknown. That is why he is usually called *Pseudo*-Dionysius, and some authors refer to him as (Pseudo-)Denys. For brevity I exclude the prefix Pseudo-, and for accuracy (and for consistency with the Greek original of his name), I will maintain the name Dionysius throughout the text.

As for the direct quotations from original works, I use the English translation of Colm Luibheid for Dionysius' works, and Andrew Louth's translation for the works of John Damscene; the English translations of Theodore the Studite are mainly mine. Regarding the citations of primary texts I identify the them by title and number as in *Patrologia graeca* (PG).

The exceptions are the *Treatises* on icons by John Damascene, which are identified as *Oratio* (I, II, or III) with the paragraph number.

# 1

## Dionysius the Areopagite in the Christian Context

### WHO WAS DIONYSIUS?

In *Epistle 1* addressed to the monk Gaius, Dionysius affirms that "this quite positively complete unknowing is knowledge of him who is above everything that is known."[1] And indeed, our knowledge of the identity of Dionysius coincides with our unknowing—we do not know anything sure about the historical person of the Areopagite. Even the denomination "Areopagite" is purely hypothetical, since our author presents himself only as Dionysius—it is from the contents of his works and from certain events told by him, that we can guess his desire to identify himself with the famous bishop of Athens, a pagan converted into Christianity by Saint Paul.

The collection of his writings, known as *Corpus Areopagiticum*, was officially mentioned for the first time by the Severian monophysites and by the bishop of Ephesus Hypatius during a meeting between the Chalcedonian and Severian monophysites, held in Constantinople in 532—the Severians used the *Corpus* as proof of the orthodoxy of their doctrines, while Hypatius expressed doubt in its authenticity.

The voice of Hypatius did not remain isolated—the assumption that the *Corpus* belonged to the Apostolic era was also questioned by Photius, Arethas, Peter the Damascene, John of Antiochia, Symeon Petritsi and others.[2]

---

1. Epistolae 1065A.

2. Hausherr, "Doutes au sujet," 484–90.

Despite these hesitations, during the entire medieval period the author of the *Corpus* had been effectively venerated as the disciple of Saint Paul and even identified with Denys, the bishop of Paris. Abbot Hilduin (ninth century) described his martyrdom in a work entitled *Passio sanctissimi Dionysii.*[3]

Only during the Renaissance, mainly thanks to the work of Lorenzo Valla and Erasmus, was the legend of Dionysius the Areopagite again put in question. It is in the light of the works of two modern scholars, Hugo Koch[4] and Josef Stiglmayr,[5] that the thesis, according to which the author of the *Corpus* belonged to the Apostolic era, was definitively abandoned. Koch and Stiglmayr established, with sufficient approximation, the chronology of the *Corpus*, although they failed to give a face to its author. Their argument rests principally on the use of Neoplatonic terms, especially concerning the problem of evil—a part of the fourth chapter of *The Divine Names* depends on *De malorum subsistentia* of Proclus. Therefore, Dionysius has to be either a contemporary of Proclus (who died in 485) or a little posterior to him. In addition, the description of the liturgy contained in the third chapter of *The Ecclesiastical Hierarchy* includes the *Creed*, which was established in 476. This fact posits our author in the period after the Chalcedon, characterized by ulterior disputes on the identity of Christ. René Roques notes:

> . . . la chronologie de Denys semble accuser l'influence de l'Henotique de l'empereur Zénon (482). Tous les passages christologiques du 'corpus' évitent en effet les formules dyophysites de Chalcédoine aussi bien que les formules d'un monophysisme intransigeant. Et cette attitude correspond parfaitement aux intentions apolémiques plusieurs fois professées par Denys.[6]

Furthermore, Dionysius is recalled by Andrew of Caesarea in his comment to the Apocalypse of John, from the end of the fifth century, and by Severus of Antiochia in a letter to Abbot John, written in 510. The

---

3. PL 106, 23–50.

4. Koch, "Proklus als Quelle," 438–54.

5. Stiglmayr, "Der Neuplatoniker Proklos als Vorlage," 253–73.

6. Roques, "Denys l'Aréopagite," 248.

period of the composition of the Corpus would, therefore, fall between 482 and the beginning of the sixth century.[7]

Despite the fact that new findings are not sufficient to determine the historical identity of Dionysius exactly, the attempts to identify him with certain known figures (e.g., Ammonius Saccas, Peter the Iberian, Peter the Fuller, Severus of Antiochia, Sergius of Reshaina, etc.) of the time (even contrary to the aforementioned dating) are frequent.

It is with certain probability that we can today retain that Dionysius was of Syriac origins, since the descriptions of the ordination of bishops, priests, and deacons in *The Ecclesiastical Hierarchy*[8] follows the section *De ordinationibus* of the Syriac liturgy, edited and translated into Latin by the Patriarch of Antiochia Ignatius Ephraem II Rahmani.[9]

Another important point of the historical-intellectual portrait of Dionysius is a Neoplatonic print, strongly felt in his writings. As a matter of fact, in *The Divine Names*,[10] he attributes to his master Hierotheus a work entitled Θεολογικαὶ στοιχειώσεις, which is the title of one of the works of Proclus Licius Diadochus. It is probable that Dionysius wanted to hide behind the name of his master the last great exponent of Neoplatonism. The veneration that the author of the *Corpus* shows for Hierotheus makes one believe that he was an enthusiastic listener of Proclus. However, not only of Proclus—some scholars have demonstrated the dependence of Dionysius on Damascius,[11] who remained the head of the school until its closure in 529. We can therefore conclude that our author was of Syriac origin and that he followed with enthusiasm the lessons of Proclus and Damascius.

At this point, we encounter another problem, which raises doubt not only concerning the person of Dionysius, but also regarding his true intentions hidden behind the *Corpus*. The abundance of Neoplatonic terms contained in his writings together with the hypothesis that he frequented the school of Athens makes one think about his religious profile and the veracity of his Christian profession—was Dionysius Christian or pagan? And further, was he a Christian initiated to the Neoplatonic doctrines

---

7. Lilla, "Introduzione," 533–35.

8. *De ecclesiastica hierarchia* 509A–B.

9. Stiglmayr, "Eine syrische Liturgie," 383–85; Lilla, "Introduzione," 535.

10. Dionysius, *De divinis nominibus* 648B.

11. For example see Roques, *L'univers dionysien*, 74.

who used the "things of the Greeks" to express the truth of the faith, or a Neoplatonist who wished to prolongate the life of the pagan thought, by introducing it into the sphere of Christian reflexion? The opinions about these questions are rather divided, and the answer cannot be but hypothetical. I myself would be more inclined to confirm Dionysius' genuine Christian sentiment and to believe that he was a convert who knew well the Neoplatonic thought. It is evident from the examination of the Corpus that the author is familiar with the patristic tradition. Moreover, it seems indisputable that his knowledge of the tradition and the experience of the Church, both in Scriptures and in liturgical practice, suggests that Dionysius participated in the ecclesiastical life and that perhaps he himself was a member of the clergy, maybe a monk. The opinion according to which this entire knowledge had been acquired just to realize an attempt to introduce pagan elements in the Christian thought seems to me too forced. After all, an attempt of this kind could easily finish as a total failure that would render vain all the effort and risk of the author of such performance.[12] It is useful here to quote Stephen Gersh, who writes:

> A careful comparison of his doctrine with that of the principle pagan Neoplatonists has convinced me: (i) That he was a genuine Christian philosopher. His transformation of paganism is too thorough to be that of pagan writer expounding Christianity. (ii) He studied at the Academy during the late fifth or early sixth cen-

12. One of the most recent publications concerning this problem is the article by Carlo Maria Mazzucchi, "Damascio, autore del *Corpus Dionysiacum*," 299–334. The main intention of Mazzucchi is to identify the author of the *Corpus* with Damascius, who presumably would have written these works in order to introduce Neoplatonic elements into Christianity. From the methodological point of view, Mazzucchi's argumentation is prevailingly historical-philological and not philosophical-theological, and it is, therefore, based on some linguistic aspects of the work (for example, pairs of names Παῦλος-Πρόκλος; Ἱερόθεος-Ἰσίδωρος; Διονύσιος-Δαμάσκιος, which have the same initials and finals, and are isosyllabic and isotonic). Further, Mazzucchi considers the events referred by Dionysius, and finds them identical with the events from the life of Damascius (eclipse of sun, Mary's funeral, and hymns). Mazzucchi's demonstrations, despite their charm, seem too forced. The only certain conclusion which can be deduced from these coincidences is that Dionsyius knew well Damascius and perhaps decided to introduce in the *Corpus* some elements of his life, which should not surprise us much since we have already established the profound admiration of Dionysius for the entire school of Athens and its masters, Proclus and Damascius, a fact that is not too difficult to grasp from the contents of his writings.

tury A.D. This dating is consistent with his apparent use of ideas found in Proclus and Damascius.[13]

Vladimir Kharlamov has nicely synthesized our knowledge about Dionysius and his *Corpus*:

> The *Corpus Dionysiacum* in its content and origin conjures up almost any meaning the word mystical can connote. It is mysterious, veiled, hidden, clandestine, concealed, arcane, esoteric, symbolic, otherworldly, and supernatural; and if one were asked to write a biography of the author, it might well be the shortest book in the world.[14]

In the end of the discussion on the true identity of the author of the *Corpus Areopagiticum* we cannot draw any sure and definite conclusion, just as Dionysius himself wished to present his own face in the key words of his work—ineffable and unknowable.[15]

## WORKS

If we follow the words of Saint Paul "Instead someone testified somewhere" (Heb 2:6), which recall a psalm of David, then we will easily understand that the question of authenticity of a text represents a subject of second order in the Christian ambit. What is really important is the contents of the text itself, and not the identity of its author. That is maybe the reason why the works of Dionysius had enormous success and why their importance has to be assessed from the point of view of the influence they exhibited.

The *Corpus Areopagiticum* consists of four works and a collection of epistles. In fifteen chapters, *The Celestial Hierarchy*, organizes, in a rigid hierarchical system regulated by precise laws, various categories of angels nominated in the Old Testament and by Saint Paul. The first three chapters serve to introduce the hierarchy, both celestial and human, and to

---

13. Gersh, *From Iamblichus to Eriugena*, 1.

14. Kharlamov, *The Beauty of the Unity*, 69.

15. Perhaps this was his real intention—to be in full accordance with the principle vein of his mysticism and to enshroud his own identity in the "cloud" of unknowing. On the other side, in the era in which he wrote it was not unusual to take a pseudonym and hide behind a famous figure, in order give greater weight to one's own ideas.

give a definition of the hierarchy and its benefits. Chapters four through ten present the celestial hierarchy by explaining the meaning of the designation "angel" and how the hierarchy is classified into three ranks, each of which is classified into three orders, proceeding from below to above. The next four chapters treat the specific problems of the hierarchy—why all the celestial beings are denominated "celestial powers"; why human hierarchs are called "angels"; why prophet Isaiah is said to have been purified by the Seraphim, and what the traditional number of angels signifies. In the end, the last chapter considers the biblical descriptions of angels.

*The Ecclesiastical Hierarchy*, in seven chapters, describes and interprets the liturgical functions and ecclesiastical orders. Each chapter considers a theme: the tradition of the ecclesiastical hierarchy and its scope; the rite of illumination; the mass and the sacrament of the Eucharist; the rite of the ointment; the ordination of bishops, priests, and deacons; the orders of the initiated and the monastic tonsure; and the funeral rites.

In thirteen chapters, the most extensive and most complex of Dionysius' writings, *The Divine Names*, examines the most significant appellatives attributed to the divinity of the Scriptures. The divinity is absolutely transcendent with respect to all the other beings, and is therefore unknowable and ineffable. The most appropriate path of approaching it is the negative one, which consists of depriving the divinity of every possible attribute, and therefore of all the appellatives. Given its transcendence, the divinity is deprived of names, yet, since it is the productive cause of beings, it can be celebrated with all the names—at the same time, it is deprived of names and endowed with many names. The second chapter introduces the basic concepts of union and distinction and clarifies that various names that celebrate the divinity refer not to the first principle, to which they are inadequate, but only to its emanations or creative powers. In the third chapter, Dionysius speaks of the importance of prayer and traces a portrait of Hierotheus. The successive chapters discuss names such as good, light, beautiful, love, ecstasy, zeal, evil,[16] being, life, wisdom, mind, word, truth, power, justice, salvation, inequality, greatness, smallness, sameness, difference, similarity, dissimilarity, rest, motion, omnipotence, "Ancient of Days," eternity, time, peace, "Holy of Holies," "King of Kings," "Lord of Lords," "God of Gods," and, in the end, perfect and one.

16. This part contains the passage from Proclus *De malorum subsistentia*, examined by Koch ("Proklus als Quelle") and Stiglmayr ("Der Neuplatoniker Proklos").

The Mystical Theology is, given its influence and importance, surprisingly brief and consists of only three chapters. Its brevity and centrality in the *Corpus* would suggest that this treatise could conveniently represent the entire system of Dionysius. On the other hand, precisely because of its density, the treatise escapes immediate comprehension and should be considered in the context of all of Areopagite's work. In *The Mystical Theology*, some crucial points of his thought are compressed in a single word or even completely omitted. The very title of the work Περὶ μυστικῆς θεολογίας could be misleading and needs to be explained. The word μυστικός used by Dionysius and other authors of his time which is usually translated as "mystic," does not mean suprarational or emotional ecstasy of extraordinary solitary individuals, but rather, it has a simpler and less technical sense of something mysterious, hidden from the others, but revealed to those who are initiated into the mysteries. As for theology, this word too has in Dionysius a special meaning—it has the literal sense of the word of God or of the Scriptures and therefore describes the intention of the Areopagite to interpret the Bible, although with a certain philosophical weight. The treatise opens with the explanation of the divine cloud and remembers that the union with God is an expression that rescinds every sensory or intellectual activity. The first chapter celebrates the negative path, speaks of the positive and negative theologies, posits the divinity above every affirmation and negation, of every word and thought, explains that the divinity appears to those who enter the cloud as happened with Moses on Sinai, and identifies the knowledge of God with ignorance. In the second chapter, Dionysius affirms that the mystical cloud is the expression of the ignorance of God and that this ignorance coincides with the highest knowledge, and specifies the roles of the positive and negative theologies—while the first proceeds from above to below, the latter follows an ascending process from below to above. In the third chapter, the discussion of affirmation and negation reaches its peak, and the entrance in the cloud is interpreted as the absolute lack of word and thought, a characteristic of the union with God. The last two chapters highlight the transcendence of the first principle with respect to every other perceptible thing and every intelligible concept.

The *Epistles* are ten and given their synthetic character, could be used as an introduction to Dionysius' thought. The *first* epistle speaks of the coincidence of the knowledge of God and the ignorance of God. The *second* affirms that God transcends every source—the first principle is beyond of the divinity and beyond of good. The *third* epistle explains that the mystery of Jesus—also the divine nature, even after the Incarnation—remains unknowable and hidden. The *fourth* letter continues the discourse of the third, establishing that Jesus is a real man, but, at the same time, remains supra-essential. The *fifth* letter resumes the argument of the cloud of unknowing. The *sixth* establishes that refuting an error does not necessarily mean comprehending the truth. In the *seventh* epistle, Dionysius speaks of the sophist Apollophanes of the eclipse of sun that happened after the death of Christ and that was observed by Dionysius himself in Heliopolis. In the *eighth* letter, the Areopagite strengthens the importance of the hierarchical order of the Church, rebuking the monk Demophilus for criticizing a priest. The *ninth* epistle speaks of the scriptural and liturgical symbolism. Finally, in the *tenth*, Dionysius foretells to Saint John the Evangelist the end of his imprisonment in Patmos.[17]

Besides these works, there are seven other Dionysius' writings about which he himself informs us, but which went lost (or maybe had never been written): 1) Περὶ νοητῶν τε καὶ αἰσθητῶν (*The Intelligible and Sensible*); 2) Θεολογικαὶ ὑποτυπώσεις (*Theological Outlines*); 3) Συμβολικὴ θεολογία (*Symbolic Theology*); 4) Θεῖοι ὕμνοι (*Divine Hymns*); 5) Περὶ τῶν ἀγγελικῶν ἰδιοτήτων καὶ τάξεων (*On the Properties and Ranks of the Angels*); 6) Περὶ δικαίου καὶ θείου δικαιωτηρίου (*On Righteous and Divine Judgment*); 7) Περὶ ψυχῆς (*On the Soul*).

## DIONYSIUS AND THE NEOPLATONIC TRADITION

The opinions that Dionysius frequented the Academy of Athens seem rather convincing. Beyond doubt, the Neoplatonic tradition found an eminent place in the *Corpus*, which is surely one of the rare Christian writings in which Neoplatonism so powerfully resounds. However, Dionysius was not the only Christian writer who studied Platonic doctrines.

We know that the master of the school of Athens had an obscure vision of the Church and of Christianity. But then, why would so many illustrious Christian scholars be attracted by this philosophical approach? Men like Justin, Origen, Clement of Alexandria, Gregory Nazianzen,

17. See Rorem, *Pseudo-Dionysius*; Lilla, "Introduzione," 537–40.

Gregory of Nissa, Basil, Augustin, Hilarius and Boethius had profound interest in Platonism.

As explained by Hathaway, it was primarily the *theologia* of Plato that the Christians wanted to hear, and this was precisely the doctrine of Proclus.[18] Plato's vision, put in the profound context of faith, retained its transparency, and "the things of the Greeks" in the hands of Dionysius and other Christian thinkers were subsumed into the vision of God offered by the Revelation.

In Dionysius, this transforming subsumption of the Platonic intuition into the Christian context reached a new form and was ultimately developed and deepened.

By carefully considering Dionysius' doctrine and, comparing it with the Neoplatonic one, we can clearly see the differences between the two. William Riordan[19] has correctly individuated four fundamental points of divergence: 1) the unity of God in Dionisyius vs. the Neoplatonic view of emanated hypostases; 2) the goodness of God's cosmos vs. the Neoplatonic doctrine, especially concerning material beings; 3) God's love for his cosmos, crucial in Dionysius, vs. different Neoplatonic doctrines, and 4) the ascent of the mystic according to Dionysius vs. the Neoplatonic ascent.

1) The famous notion of "emanating hypostases" is an attempt of the Neoplatonists to express how the transcendent One can, in certain manner, become immanent. From the absolute and transcendent One "pours forth," emanates (ἀπορρέω) a series of forms, called hypostases, each of which, through its own excess (ὑπερβολή or περιουσία), generates another successive hypostasis. These hypostases initially proceed in groups of three (triads). According to Plotinus, the triad includes the following three hypostases: the *One*, from which proceeds *Intelligence*, from which proceeds *Soul*.[20] For Proclus each of these generates replicas—from the One, "henades" or gods; from Intelligence, intelligences, or demons, or angels; from the Soul, souls. These replicas also generate in "threes": three orders of henades, three orders of intelligences, three orders of souls. In addition to a *procession* of these nine levels of emanated beings, Proclus

18. Hathaway, *Hierarchy and the Definition of Order*, 20.

19. Riordan, *Divine Light*, 77.

20. Roques, *L'univers*, 70–71.

also identifies a *rest* of the emanated ones and a *return* back, within each of these sub-triads, to the originating principle of each, and in the end, a return back of all to the One. Each member of each triad is caused by a higher member of the triad.[21] Every effect therefore proceeds, rests within, and returns to its cause. Each new level, being an effect of the previous level, represents a new procession. The triad One-Intelligence-Soul, in its tripartite relations, is imitated by each of its own sub-hypostases; the henades that generate from the One imitate it; the intelligences that generate from Intelligence, imitate it, and the souls that generate from the Soul, imitate it. Therefore, the whole of all successive hypostases proceed, rest, and return from the One, through the One, and within the One.

The excess of the One and consequently the "pouring forth" of Intelligence and Soul according to the Neoplatonic doctrine happen out of certain necessity. For Dionysius, on the contrary, God is completely and absolutely One and so are all the attributes (i.e., all the divine names and all the perfections of all creatures) in the identity of His own simplicity.[22] As a matter of fact, every treatment of the divine names for Dionysius is an occasion to reaffirm the identity of all that concerns unity, goodness, light, etc., in a single principle—God. What the Neoplatonists would call three triads (One-Intelligence-Soul) for the Areopagite is simply God, and not a series of emanations. Hence, what for the Neoplatonists was an ineffable One followed by a series of gods, for Dionysius becomes the Christian God with a plurality of divine attributes.[23]

2)    The considerations on matter lead one to conclude that, according to the Neoplatonic view, it has an evil character or, in the best of cases, a negligible value. The necessity of the cosmos (i.e. the necessity that it proceeds) adds the inevitable deterioration inherent in the series of progressively descending emanations and leads the Neoplatonists to definitely refute the matter. Since matter is mutable and corruptible, it is seen as the source of evil. Souls—emanated from the good

---

21. Each member remains within its own subtriad—"All things are in all things, but in each according to its proper nature" (Proclus, *Elements of Theology* 103).

22. Riordan, *Divine Light*, 81–83.

23. Gersh, *From Iamblichus to Eriugena*, 11.

hypostasis, from the Soul—have therefore passed into the form of matter. On the one side, the body is good, since it is a distant image of the intelligible realities in the Intelligence, but on the other, it is in some way evil, given its mutable character. In the end, Plotinus, however, sees the sinfulness as a necessary result of the carnal aspect of man.

For the Neoplatonists, the world does not have origin in the creative act of God who wishes out of love to share His goodness with other beings. On the contrary, Plotinus and his successors speak of the eternal cosmos, which does not come out of love, but out of necessity and through a chain of emanations. For Dionysius, God is the creative Cause of everything, including sensible creatures. Every being immediately proceeds from His creative act, which provides being to creatures, and "comes to abide within all things". Evil should be seen as a lack of the fullness of being and not as the derivation of the Principle of all, God.[24]

In order to describe the procession of creatures from God, Dionysius uses the term πρόοδος, which was used by Neoplatonists to indicate the emanations. God is the principle of all the creatures and endows them with the capacity of being and acting. This would also include the historical acts of God (e.g., inspiration of prophets through special visions) with the scope to bring His cosmos, through these salvific acts, to the perfection that was from the beginning projected by God. The Neoplatonic One does not accomplish individual historical acts. His cosmos, as said before, proceeds out of necessity and through a descending chain of emanated hypostases. The Neoplatonic notion implies a vision of the world as necessary, as an eternal "queue" that devolves from the One.[25]

God, according to Dionysius, is providential. The expression πρόνοια indicates a Being that knows and loves those whom He creates, and it would be doubtful to say that the Neoplatonic One has any kind of direct knowledge of the particular beings. In Dionysius, we find an intimate divine Providence. And so it is that as Cause of all and as transcending all, he is rightly nameless and yet has the

---

24. Riordan, *Divine Light*, 90.

25. Ibid.

names of everything that is. Truly, he has dominion over all, and all things revolve around him, for he is their cause, their source, and their destiny. He is "all in all," as scripture affirms, and certainly, he is to be praised as being for all things the creator and originator, the One who brings them to completion, their preserver, their protector, their home, and the power that returns them to itself, and all this in the one single, irrepressible, and supreme act. For the unnamed goodness is not just the cause of cohesion or life or perfection so that it is from this or that providential gesture that it earns a name, but it actually contains everything beforehand within itself—and this in an uncomplicated and boundless manner—and it is thus by virtue of the unlimited goodness of its single all creative Providence. Hence, the songs of praise and the names for it are fittingly derived from the sum total of creation.[26]

3) In Dionysius, we can note an intimate involvement of God with His cosmos, an involvement completely extraneous to the Neoplatonic One. As Dionysius says, "The very cause of the universe in the beautiful, good superabundance of his benign yearning for all is also carried outside of himself in the loving care he has for everything . . . and is enticed away from his transcendent dwelling place and comes to abide within all things."[27] In a similar way, Proclus, too, speaks of eros that descends from above, from the sphere of intelligibles to the sphere of man, but for Dionysius, it is the very Absolute One, and not eros, that descends from above. The Tearchy of Dionsysius, prepossessing in Itself all the perfections (which for Proclus are only the emanated processions), is capable of an immediate presence in His creatures.[28] This erotic presence and the union of the One with the material being of His cosmos are relations completely extraneous to Neoplatonism.

4) For Dionysius, as well for the Neoplatonic tradition, the ascent of the mystic plays an important role. The mystic is seen as a chosen person who accomplishes the climb to the One. According to Plotinus, this

---

26. Dionysius, *De divinis nominibus* 596C–597A.

27. Dionysius, *De divinis nominibus* 712A–B.

28. Riordan, *Divine Light*, 94.

is the "flight" (ascent) to "the Fatherland" (the One). Main points of divergence between the Dionysian and Plotinian views consist of different considerations of the soul and differences regarding the method of the ascent. While for Plotinus, the main task of the soul is to restore the state in which it was before being generated by the One (since the soul is equal to the One, but in an inferior form), for Dionysius the return (ἐπιστροφή) to God does not include a "re-amalgamation" with the One. According to the Areopagite, the soul is a being created in the image of God, and it is therefore a created image and not an emanation of the eternal soul. As for the method, Plotinus considers the ascent a solitary enterprise of the soul, and there is no proof of a certain interest of the One in the ascent. In Dionysius, the ascent consists of cooperation—the mystic is, from the beginning to the end, moved by God, and not only: the soul is assisted in many ways by other beings involved in the deification, i.e. other men and angels. The soul is not alone, but it is a part of an enormous, splendid symphony of beings disposed in a double order, celestial and ecclesiastical. These dynamic orders for the deification of intelligible beings cooperate with God in His work. The endeavor of the soul is also directed towards the good of other souls in their ascent, and vice versa.[29] Furthermore, the notions of dark and cloud, so important in Dionysius, are absent from the mystical ascent of Plotinus. For the Areopagite, this cloud, which is the excessive light of the divine Being, is precisely where the mystic needs to dwell (διατριβῇ). The Christian mystic needs to put himself in the hands of God in order to receive the work of God: the ascent (ἀναγογία) is more a "being-uplifted" in cooperation with God than a solitary climb.[30] Finally, the ecstasy in Dionysius means to go forth from being, while ecstasy of Plotinus means to reduce the being to an absolute simplicity.[31]

---

29. For example, "When we talk of love, whether this be in God or an angel, in the mind or in the spirit or in nature, we should think of a unifying and co-mingling power which moves the superior to provide for the subordinate, peer to be in communion with peer, and subordinate to return to the superior and the outstanding." (Dionysius, *De divinis nominibus* 713A–B).

30. Roques, *L'univers*, 130; Riordan, *Divine Light*, 109–11.

31. Lossky, *The Mystical Theology of the Eastern Church*, 30.

## THE NEGATIVE AND POSITIVE THEOLOGIES AND THE CHARACTERISTICS OF THE DIVINITY[32]

The negative theology (apophatic method) consists of depriving the first principle of every possible attribute, while the positive theology (cataphatic method) attributes the divinity with every property. These two theologies represent for Dionysius two ways that lead to the divinity— the negative theology considers the divinity in its absolute transcendence (μονή) and affirms its difference from beings, and the positive theology considers it as the cause of all beings,[33] i.e., as the principle from which all beings proceed in virtue of the πρόοδος. These two paths have opposite directions—the positive theology paces, through πρόοδος, a descending process from the divinity to the beings, while the negative theology has an ascending character, i.e. rises from beings to the first principle.[34] That is why the divinity is deprived of names and the object of all possible names at the same time.[35]

The method of the two theologies reminds one of applying to the divinity the negative and positive concepts contained in the first and second hypotheses of Plato's *Parmenides*, which is the basis of Neoplatonic theology. Therefore, these two ways do not differ only on a methodological level, but also on an ontological level, as expressions of the ambit of being and of the ambit of non-being. The first, negative hypothesis refers

---

32. It is important here to note that "apophatic theology" and "negative theology" are not quite synonymous. The latter does not perceive the positive element of apophatic thinking that was ultimately lost in the Western *theologia negativa*—the apophatic theology does not mean an agnosticism or an absolute denial of the possibility to know God; on the contrary, there is "what is known about God," what is searchable and provable, but these elements do not lay upon human logic—they are taught by the Holy Spirit. I will use the terms negative/positive theology throughout the book only for linguistic simplicity. (On this see Bergmann, *Creation Set Free*, esp. 339ff.; and Radovic, *Το μυστήριον*, esp. the first chapter.)

33. Dionysius, *De divinis nominibus* 593B; and Dionysius, *De mystica theologia* 1000B.

34. Dionysius, *De mystica theologia* 1025B.

35. Dionysius, *De divinis nominibus* 596A–C. A similar doctrine is found in the *Corpus Hermeticum*: "This is the God superior to any name, this is He who is not evident to the senses and who, in the same time, is evident in highest degree . . . And that is why it has every name, since all things proceed from this only Father, and in the same time it has no name, since it is the Father of all things" (CH, V:10).

to μονή, and the second, positive hypothesis refers to πρόοδος.[36] Precisely this approach allowed Dionysius, as Corsini writes, to actuate the conciliation between Christianity and pagan philosophy, to which the Fathers of the Church prior to him, were so inclined. On the one hand, this distinction between an unknowable transcendence and a total immanence saved the Dionysian doctrine from every possible accusation of pantheism, and on the other, it allowed Dionysius to assimilate all the positive aspects of human reason's elaboration on God.[37] Further, by insisting on the absolute impossibility of our knowing God outside His exterior manifestations, the Areopagite succeeded in overcoming all the doctrinal controversies within Christianity, thus making unjustified the existence of such quarrels.

The mental structure described in the writings that deal with positive and negative theologies could be resumed as a descending sequence of affirmations, which proceeds downward and increases in size with the extent of the descent, accompanied by an ascending sequence of negations, which returns upward and decreases with the extent of the ascent. At the end of this ascending negative sequence, it reaches the point of silence and union with the ineffable. The relation of this structure with the philosophical frame of procession and return is evident. The parallel between the descent of affirmations and the divine procession from simplicity to plurality of this world, and between the ascent of negations and the return to the union with God, does not have a function of the objective ontology, but of the subjective epistemology. The entire endeavor of Dionysius is a cognitive exercise, dominated by the right interpretation of the names and symbols of God, both in Bible and in liturgy, and culminated by the intentional abandon of all similar interpretations.[38]

Although both theologies are acceptable and legitimate, the Areopagite considers the negative theology more adequate to the unknowable nature of the first principle. In *The Celestial Hierarchy*, speaking of biblical exegesis, Dionysius affirms that God is represented by names that designate not what He is, but what He is not,[39] and retains that this negative way is the most appropriate one. In *The Divine Names*, too, it is

36. See Lilla, "Introduzione," 545–46.

37. Corsini, *Il trattato*, 78.

38. Rorem, *Pseudo-Dionysius*, 200.

39. Dionysius, *De coelesti hierarchia* 140D.

said that the preference of the sacred authors is "for the way up through negations, since this stands the soul outside everything which is correlative with its own finite nature."[40] The apophatic theology will have great success in the patristic thought, but also in the contemporary experience of the Church. Many authors will reaffirm the importance of negations. As Lossky says:

> Negative theology is not merely a theory of ecstasy. It is an expression of that fundamental attitude which transforms the whole of theology into a contemplation of the mysteries of revelation . . . Apophaticism teaches us to see above all a negative meaning in the dogmas of the Church: it forbids us to follow natural ways of thought and to form concepts which would usurp the place of spiritual realities . . . The apophatic attitude gave to the Fathers of the Church that freedom and liberality with which they employed philosophical terms without running the risk of being misunderstood or of falling into a theology of concepts.[41]

Two principal characteristics of the divinity, in the doctrine of Dionysius, are the absolute transcendence of the divinity and its immanence in the universe, referred to as μονή and πρόοδος, respectively. The first characteristic follows from the application of negative concepts of the first Parmenidean hypothesis to μονή. The most characteristic motifs of the divine transcendence are:

1. God is bereaved of form and is untouchable;

2. God is superior to all beings;

3. God does not conform to any being;

4. God is superior to the being;

5. God is a non-being;

6. God is superior to the intelligence;

7. God is superior to thought and to knowledge—therefore, He is absence of thought, He is unknowable, and all the possible knowledge of Him coincide with ignorance;

---

40. Dionysius, *De divinis nominibus* 981B.
41. Lossky, *The Mystical Theology*, 42.

8. God is superior to the word and therefore ineffable, deprived of names and superior to any name;

9. God is superior to any state, and to any affirmation or negation;

10. God is superior to the infinity and to the limit;

11. God is at the same time identical to the infinity in a triple sense (encloses in itself everything potentially, is provided with an infinite number of potencies and is unknown); and

12. God is superior to time and to eternity.[42]

Most of these conclusions are found in *The Divine Names*, and some in *The Mystical Theology*.

In the second moment, in πρόοδος, which is together providential and creative, the divinity traverses all, reaches all beings and is, therefore, immanent in the universe. Such a procession, which becomes a transmission (διάδοσις, χορηγία), happens after the overflow (ἐκβλύζειν, ὑπερβλύζειν) of the infinite potency (δύναμις) of which God is extremely full (ὑπερπλήρης).[43] It represents the movement of God, the supreme law of the universe and its peace, so to say that it is the cause of the harmony that pervades it and of the communion of beings among them.[44] Furthermore, it ties the center of the universe with the extremities and embraces (περιέχει) and holds together (συνέχει) everything.[45]

Although God is the super-essential One, He is also the Trinity. All the divine names of God nominate the Trinity too, since God is "the tearchical essence" (τὴν θεαρχικὴν ὅλην ὕπαρξιν).[46] What belongs to One of these Three belongs to all. In *The Divine Names*, Dionysius writes: "Indeed, it seems to me that only through perversity would anyone, reared on Holy Scripture, deny that the attributes of God refer in all their truth and meaning to the complete Divinity." Reaching the "most beautiful canon of the truth" (κανόνα κάλλιστον ἀληθείας),[47] we will find that to the complete

---

42. Lilla, "Introduzione," 547.

43. For example, Dionysius, *De coelesti hierachia* 177C; Dionysius, *De divinis nominibus* 892B, 956B, 977B.

44. Dionysius, *De divinis nominibus* 892C–893A; 948D–952B.

45. Lilla, "Introduzione," 548.

46. Dionysius, *De divinis nominibus* 636C.

47. Dionysius, *De divinis nominibus* 637C–640B.

Divinity belong the unified names such as "super-good" (τὸ ὑπεράγαθον) or "super-divine" (τὸ ὑπέρθεον). In God, there are union and distinction ineffable in unity. God is infinity of His perfections, which differ from each other, in the absolute simplicity of the One. The names of His perfections nominate the complete Divinity.

Distinguished are the super-essential name and the reality of the Father, the Son, and the Holy Spirit, since "they cannot be interchanged, nor are they held in common," but according to the Scriptures, there are certain specific unities and differentiations within the unity and differentiation, as discussed above. Thus, regarding the divine unity beyond being, they assert that the indivisible Trinity holds within a shared undifferentiated unity its super-essential subsistence, its super-divine divinity, its super-excellent goodness, its supremely individual identity beyond all that is, its oneness beyond the source of oneness, its ineffability, its many names, its unknowability, its wholly belonging to the conceptual realm, the assertion of all things, the denial of all things, that which is beyond every assertion and denial, and finally, if one may put it so, the abiding and foundation of the divine persons who are the source of oneness as a unity that is totally undifferentiated and transcendent.[48] Dionysius illustrates this meaning by an image of a room in which there are three lamps. Their light, in the air, is one, while the lamps remain to be three, and in the same way, for the three persons "there is unity in distinction, and there is distinction in unity."[49] In another passage, Dionysius identifies the Father with the original Divinity, while "the Son and the Spirit are, so to speak, divine offshoots, the flowering and transcendent lights of the divinity."[50] The Father is the principle of the Son and of the Spirit; each of the divine Persons, in the unity of the indivisible divine Being, is not either of the other two Persons. Each of the three Persons, however, is the totality of the divine Being and possesses the fullness of all the divine perfections.[51]

---

48. Dionysius, *De divinis nominibus* 640C–641A.

49. Dionysius, *De divinis nominibus* 641B–C.

50. Dionysius, *De divinis nominibus* 645B.

51. See Riordan, *Divine Light*, 134–35.

## THE LAWS OF THE HIERARCHIES AND THE ASCENT OF THE MIND TO GOD

For Dionysius there are two worlds—one of the pure intelligences and one of the incarnated intelligences. The first represents the celestial hierarchy and the second the ecclesiastical hierarchy. These two worlds, however, are not absolutely separated, and, as a matter of fact, the second is the image of the first. The hierarchies, as described in the works of Dionysius, suggest that the sensible and intelligible reigns are not reached by a single being, but by a plurality of beings of different kinds, and that the vision of God is transmitted from one being to another in a descendant manner, through the ranks of the hierarchies.

At the peak of the scale stand the superior angelic orders—their perfection is determined by the privileged level of their communication with God. According to the pure spirituality of their nature, they are closest to God and are therefore, mediators in His revelation to the world, messengers of His will and of His mysteries. This service is in fact the expression of the name "angel," which belongs to the entire superior world; in a strict sense, it is just a name of one of the celestial orders. The celestial world is itself organized in a hierarchical manner, and not all the angelic orders receive equally the divine illumination—the inferior orders receive the illumination from the superior orders.[52] Therefore, a general division of the celestial hierarchy would include the most divine sacraments represented by the completely immaterial knowledge of God and of divine things; the divine beings who know these sacraments and are its initiators, represented by the first angelic essences; and those who are sacredly initiated by the latter, represented by the inferior essences. These three terms (i.e., sacraments, initiators, and initiated) are equally found in the ecclesiastical hierarchy.[53]

The doctrine of the Church on nine angelic levels is divided by Dionysius in three triadic groups, i.e., in three hierarchies each of which is constituted of three orders, each of which contains three ranks of powers: first, second, and last. The ecclesiastical hierarchy has an analogous constitution, but contains only two triads: the sacerdotal hierarchy, divided in three orders, and the hierarchy of the initiated, also divided in

52. Florovsky, *Vizantiskie otsi V–VIII vekov*, 112–13.

53. See Roques, *L'univers*, 68–70.

three orders. Each of the intelligences of each of the ecclesiastical orders represents a triad, since it carries three ranks of powers: first, median, and last. The nine orders of angels, divided in three hierarchical orders, are as follows: thrones, cherubims, seraphims (first rank); authorities, powers, dominions (second rank); angels, archangels, principalities (third order). The first rank of the ecclesiastical hierarchy consists of bishops, priests and deacons, while the second rank is formed by three orders of initiated: those being purified, illuminated and perfect. Those being purified (cathecumens, penitents and possessed) are entrusted to deacons, the illuminated (holy people) to priests, and the perfect (monks or therapists) to bishops.[54]

Since the two hierarchies are not separated, but closely connected, there have to be common points, or better, laws that regulate both hierarchies. Lilla has divided these laws into sixteen points:

1.    The ecclesiastical hierarchy is an imitation of the celestial one.

2.    Superior members of the hierarchy receive the divine ray directly from God in proportion to their capacities, and reflect it towards the inferior members.

3.    There is a close connection between the hierarchical rank of each being and its capacity to receive the divine light.

4.    Superior members purify, illuminate, and perfect inferior members thus imitating God, the principle of every purification, illumination, and perfection. The same functions are realized in the ecclesiastical hierarchy by superior members with respect to the inferior.

5.    Superior members of the hierarchy "initiate" the inferiors, i.e., impart to them a genuine esoteric teaching. The same thing happens in the ecclesiastical hierarchy.

6.    Angels reveal and transmit the arcane of the divinity.

7.    In single ranks of the hierarchy the angelic essences are as well ordered hierarchically.

---

54. See Rorem, *Pseudo-Dionysius*, esp. 67 and 96.

8.  While superior orders possess all the properties of inferior orders, the latter possess only partially the properties of superior orders.

9.  In the hierarchy are to be distinguished two moments of participation and transmission: while the participation indicates the relation of inferior beings to superior, the transmission indicates the providence of superior beings with respect to the inferior.

10. The initiation, perfect at its origin, becomes paler and paler as it proceeds towards inferior orders.

11. The knowledge of the divinity proper of the higher rank is clearer than the level of initiation reached by intermediate members.

12. The process of initiation becomes more and more manifest down the hierarchical scale: the revelatory function of the second hierarchy is more manifest than the one of the first and is more hidden than the one of the last, which reveals what is closest to the world.

13. The lowest angelic order instructs and protects the human hierarchy.

14. Major or minor rank of participation in the divine light depends only on major or minor aptitude of beings to receive it, and not on the nature of the light, which always remains the same.

15. The only divine providence entrusted the protection of various nations of the world to the respective angels.

16. The divine power connects the extremities of the hierarchies and unites superior members with inferior and inferior with superior through the transmission of power and conversion, respectively.[55]

The scope of life is the communication with God, the deification, and this is as well the scope of the existence of hierarchies—hierarchy is the realizer of the deification.

Angelic orders, whose scope is to reveal the secret knowledge of the divinity, make possible the ascent of the human mind to God, them be-

55. Lilla, "Introduzione," 554–57.

ing true intermediaries between man and God. The lowest order of the celestial hierarchy, represented by real angels, uplifts man transmitting to him their own illuminations received by higher orders. Archangels generously announce to angels the illuminations received by first powers, and then, through angels, announce it to us.[56] Angels are the point of contact with humanity in the work of mediated revelation—this happens because "the uplifting and return toward God, and the communion and union, might occur according to proper order."[57] There is a twofold movement proceeding from God: the vast procession of beings from God and the attractive force that initiates, maintains and completes their return back to Him. The deification operated by God through His hierarchies assimilates each member of each order to the Being of God. Each becomes more similar to God through a deepened perfection of its own being. In the process of participation, each becomes more divine and so distributes its own procession, transmitting the divine Being to inferior beings. All the beings, according to their position in the hierarchies, participate in the πρόοδος and in the ἐπιστροφή of God, through their own πρόοδος and ἐπιστροφή. Thus, the entire hierarchical cosmos of creatures cooperates with God towards the culmination of the entire matter.[58] Louis Bouyer notes:

> It is fundamental that the various degrees of the hierarchy, or rather of the Dionysian hierarchies, are simply so many relays for communicating what the higher beings can keep for themselves only by sharing freely with others (as pseudo-Dionysius explicitly asserts). And though these others can receive the gift from above only in proportion to their capacity, it is still the gift of God, i.e. not only something he gives, but in the final analysis his very self. This is what Endre von Ivanka, among others, has established, in contrast to many superficial commentators. And the insight follows logically from the central Dionysian assertion that, through creation, the created hierarchies are but the communication and extension of the uncreated thearchy, i.e. of the eternal exchange between the divine persons.[59]

56. Rorem, *Pseudo-Dionysius*, 67.

57. Dionysius, *De coelesti hierarchia* 260B.

58. Riordan, *Divine Light*, 52–53.

59. Bouyer, *Cosmos*, 200.

The thearchy with the cosmic hierarchies could be represented with the following diagram:

| | | |
|---|---|---|
| THEARCHY | Father<br>Son<br>Holy Spirit | |
| CELESTIAL HIERARCHY | Seraphim<br>Cherubim<br>Thrones | 1st angelic triad |
| | Dominations<br>Virtes<br>Powers | 2nd angelic triad |
| | Principalities<br>Archangels<br>Angels | 3rd angelic triad |
| ECCLESIASTICAL HIERARCHY | Hierarchs (bishops)<br>Priests<br>Deacons | 1st ecclesiastical triad |
| | Monks<br>Faithful<br>Those being purified | 2nd ecclesiastical triad |
| SUBHUMAN HIERARCHY | Animals<br>Plants<br>Minerals | subhuman triad |

As previously stated, the absolute transcendence of the μονή implies, as consequence, the knowledge of God coincides with ignorance. In *The Mystical Theology*, this ignorance is indicated as a result of the negative theology, which is the most adequate way of approaching the first principle in rational terms:

I pray we could come to this darkness so far above light! If only we lacked sight and knowledge so as to see, so as to know, un-seeing and unknowing, that which lies beyond all vision and knowledge. For this would be really to see and to know: to praise the Transcendent One in a transcending way, namely through the denial of all beings. We would be like sculptors who set out to carve a statue. They remove every obstacle to the pure view of the hidden image, and simply by this act of clearing aside. they show up the beauty which is hidden.[60]

To follow the negative way, one should go in an ascending direc-tion—while affirmations represent the descending *procession* of God in our conceptual and perceptive world, negations are our ascending *return* from perception and knowledge to God. This ascending path, on which we gradually free ourselves from the dominion of what is accessible to knowledge, Dionysius compares with the ascent of Moses on mount Sinai:

But then he [Moses] breaks free of them, away from what sees and is seen, and he plunges into the truly mysterious darkness of unknowing. Here, renouncing all that the mind may conceive, wrapped entirely in the intangible and the invisible, he belongs completely to him who is beyond everything. Here, being neither oneself nor someone else, one is supremely united to the com-pletely unknown by an inactivity of all knowledge, and knows beyond the mind by knowing nothing.[61]

It becomes clear that the apophatic way has no object—the word "breaks free of them, away from what sees and is seen" means to free oneself of both the subject and object of one's perception. God does not represent the object, since what we deal with here is not knowledge, but union. The negative theology is therefore a path towards the mystical union with God, whose nature remains forever unknown.[62] Such a mysti-cal union is based on a direct relationship between the human mind and the source of light that excludes the intervention of intermediary angels, who are in fact dispensers of esoteric knowledge. Despite that, they be-long to the rational sphere, while the ἕνωσις of the human mind with

60. Dionysius, *De mystica theologia* 1025B.
61. Dionysius, *De mystica theologia* 1001A.
62. Lossky, *The Mystical Theology*, 28.

the sum principle is characterized by cessation and overcoming of every noetic function.[63]

In the end of the apophatic way, not only affirmations, but also negations are being negated, since they too are human concepts and therefore cannot comprehend the infinity and transcendence of God. During the ascent, the literary and conceptual discourse diminishes from expansive interpretation to terse negations, and in the end, it ceases completely, disappearing in the cloud of unknowing. The union with God is reached, but this union cannot be described, not even in a negative way.[64] In the last words of *The Mystical Theology*, God "is beyond every denial,"[65] negation is negated and the human mind passes into silence. In the end, only the silence remains.

63. Lilla, "Introduzione," 565.

64. Rorem, *Pseudo-Dionysius*, 193–94, 213.

65. Dionysius, *De mystica theologia* 1048B.

# 2

## The Historical-Doctrinal Development
## of the Iconoclastic Controversy

### HISTORY

One of the greatest disputes in the history of Christianity is, beyond all doubt, the iconoclastic controversy, which was not only a philosophical-theological debate, but also one with profound historical-political implications.

The iconoclastic crisis was announced during the brief reign of Emperor Philippikos (711–713), who was of Armenian origin. Given his origin, the Emperor was probably inclined to monophysism, although he had not tried to institutionalize it officially. However, he was a fervid defender of monothelitism—he refuted the decisions of the Sixth Ecumenical Council and proclaimed monothelitism as the only acceptable doctrine. This attitude found its symbolic expression in the destruction of the image of the Council in the imperial palace, and in the deletion of the inscription on the gate before the palace, which was replaced with images of the Emperor and Patriarch Sergius, founder of monothelitism.

The new ecclesiastic policy of the Emperor found a strong opposition in Rome, thus creating a tension that was expressed in a symbolic manner, again through the use of images. As a matter of fact, Philippikos sent to the pope his monothelite Creed and one of his images. In Rome, the image of the heretical emperor was rejected and was not incised on coins, while his name was omitted from the prayers. Since the Emperor removed the image of the Sixth Council, the pope decided to put inside Saint Peter's cathedral images of all six ecumenical councils.

On June 3, 713, Philippikos was assassinated in a conspiracy of the court, and his secretary Artemius (Anastasius III) was crowned as the new emperor. The first decision made by Anastasius was the solemn proclamation of the Sixth Ecumenical Council—the image of the Council, removed by Philippikos, was put back in its old place, while the images of Philippikos and Sergius were destroyed.[1]

Iconoclasm, in its proper form, had its beginning with the Emperor Leo III (717–741), who was of Syrian origin[2] and for many years lived in the oriental provinces of the empire, where the iconoclastic stream was very strong. In 726, Leo openly declared himself against the cult of images,[3] probably influenced by a visit of the bishops from Asia Minor,[4] but also by a strong earthquake, which he interpreted as a sign of the rage of God, provoked by the veneration of images. In the beginning, the Emperor preached to his people, trying to convince them that the icons were contrary to the Christian doctrines; this was his understanding of the imperial power bestowed upon him by God—βασιλεὺς καὶ ἱερεύς εἰμι ("I am both Emperor and priest"), he would write some years later in a letter addressed to the pope.

Shortly after the Emperor's preachings, an imperial officer removed the image of Christ from the Bronze Gate of the imperial palace. However, this place did not remain empty—Leo III replaced the image of Christ with a cross and put an inscription beneath it: The Lord does not allow a portrait of Christ to be drawn without voice, deprived of breath, made of earthly matter, which is despised by Scripture. Therefore, Leo III, with his son, the new Constantine, engraved on the gates of the kings the blessed prototype of the cross, the glory of the faithful.[5]

---

1. Ostrogorski, *Istorija Vizantije*, 162–63.

2. Many scholars see in this the true background of the iconoclastic controversy—the oriental origins of Leo III are supposed to be the causes of his policy, due to the influence of Monophysitism, Islam and Judaism in Middle-Eastern regions (See for example Grabar, *L'iconoclasme byzantine*).

3. Τούτῳ τῷ ἔτει ἤρξατο ὁ δυσσεβὴς βασιλεὺς Λέων τῆς κατὰ τῶν ἁγίων καὶ σεπτῶν εἰκόνων καθαιρέσεως λόγον ποιεῖσθαι (Theophanes, *Chronographia*, I, 621, 6–8).

4. See Ostrogorsky, "Le début de la Qurelle des Images," 235.

5. Cited in Besançon, *The Forbidden Image*, 124.

If Leo III wanted to verify the mood of his people, he must have been disappointed: the rage of the citizens was such that the officer was immediately killed. However, the uprising had a major impact in Greece—on the news of the new iconoclastic policy, the theme Hellas turned against Leo, proclaimed its own emperor and directed its fleet towards Constantinople.[6] So, at the very beginning, the position of the European parts of the empire was clear, and it would be evident during the entire process of the dispute. The Emperor, however, shortly thereafter succeeded in succumbing the uprising, but the rebellion of an entire province meant a very serious alarm.

Despite his iconoclastic zeal, Leo III acted cautiously at first. Only in the tenth year of his reign did he decide to declare himself against icons, and only a few years later did he promulgate the iconoclastic edict. Those were the years of negotiation with ecclesiastic authorities—the emperor was trying to gain the support of the Patriarch of Constantinople and the pope of Rome, but Patriarch Germanos showed a strong opposition to the iconoclastic tendencies, and, furthermore, the correspondence with Pope Gregory II was likewise unsuccessful.

Since the negotiations failed on all sides, the Emperor had no other choice, but to use force; he did, however, try to ensure at least an ostensible legality of his positions and on January 17, 730, he convoked the assembly of secular and ecclesiastic dignitaries, with the scope to promulgate an edict against the cult of images. Germanos refused to sign the document, and, as a consequence, was deposed from the patriarchal throne. His successor, Anastasius, followed the imperial orders, and so the iconoclastic doctrine acquired the legal force, thus initiating a systematic destruction of icons and a persecution of their venerators.[7]

After Leo's death, his son, Constantine V (741–775) was heir to the imperial throne. During his campaign against the Arabs in 742, his brother-in-law Artabasdos usurped the throne. Many public officers sided with Artabasdos, who received the imperial crown from the hands of Patriarch Anastasios. It seems that the iconoclastic policy found no unanimous support even among the closest associates of Constantine— with the coronation of Artabasdos, the cult of images was re-established

---

6. Ostrogorski, *Istorija Vizantije*, 170.
7. Ostrogorski, *Istorija Vizantije*, 172.

in Constantinople. This usurpation of the throne, however, lasted for a short time and already in 743, Constantine V managed to enter the capital and regain his throne. Artabasdos was blinded, while Anastasios, after a public humiliation, remained on the patriarchal throne.

Constantine decided to reinforce his iconoclastic policy with an ecclesiastic council. In order to prepare a favorable decision of such council, he assigned the episcopal thrones to his followers and founded new dioceses, which he entrusted to the exponents of iconoclasm. The Emperor also initiated doctrinal debates between the two parties, but the iconodules often ended in prisons, where they had to remain during the council. The literary polemics on the doctrine was not reserved only for ecclesiastic doctors, but the Emperor himself took part in the dispute— he wrote thirteen theological treatises, of which only two survived in fragments.

The council was convoked on February 10, 754, in the imperial palace in Hiereia, and was officially closed on August 8, in Constantinople. The council gathered 338 bishops who were all willing to accept the iconoclastic doctrine. The sessions of the council were presided by bishop Theodosios of Ephesus, since Patriarch Anastasius was already dead and the pope and eastern Patriarchs did not send their representatives. Despite this fact, the council proclaimed itself ecumenical and declared against any type of veneration of images of religious character. The decisions, announced at the main square of Constantinople, ordered the destruction of all icons, anathematized the exponents of the Iconodule party, and declared punishable every respect for icons. It is curious here to ask when, according to the iconoclastic bishops, the idolatry started within the Church. Since they proclaimed their council ecumenical, they accepted all six previous ecumenical councils,[8] which meant that the Church of that period was still pure and uncorrupted. This would suggest that the idolatrous practice penetrated the Church between 681 and 726, which is very hard to accept as a genuine iconoclastic position.[9]

The realization of these decisions was opposed by the representatives of the iconophile party, led by Abbot Stephen, who, after long fights, was tortured and murdered on the streets of Constantinople in 765.[10] A

8. See Mansi XIII:221C–D.

9. Schönborn, *God's Human Face*, 146–47.

10. Ostrogorski, *Istorija Vizantije*, 180–81.

stronger opposition to the imperial policy found its representatives in monastic orders, and so the fight against iconodules transformed into a fight against monks. Monks were constrained to renounce monastic life, monasteries were closed or transformed in military stations, and their goods confiscated. A radical example of such attitude was the act of the strategos of Ephesus, Michael Lachanodrakon, who constrained monks to parade in the robe of a bridegroom, i.e., to replace the monastic schema with a garment that a man wore when he was finally committed to marriage.[11] Constantine had the famous representation of the six ecumenical councils in the Milion of Constantinople replaced by a depiction of the hippodrome games, on which he even had his favorite charioteer depicted.[12] The Emperor did not limit himself just to the destruction of icons, but also prohibited the cult of the Virgin and of saints. It was only with the death of Constantine V that this radical policy had its end.

The reign of Constantine's son and successor Leo IV the Khazar (775-780), apart from being brief, was also marked by a moderated policy concerning the iconoclastic doctrine. The new Emperor renounced the cruel methods of his father and interrupted the persecutions of monks, some of whom even became metropolitans. Leo IV was probably influenced by his wife Irene, who, born in Athens, supported the iconophile party. When her husband died, Irene took over the imperial role, since the son Constantine VI, heir of the throne, was only twelve years old.

In 784, Irene openly expressed her position on images—Patriarch Paul, nominated during the reign of Leo IV, resigned and his place was taken by Tarasius, Irene's personal secretary. She also dismissed many experienced military commanders (such as the aforementioned strategos Michael Lachanodrakon), replacing them with inexperienced commanders who would support her intention to end iconoclasm.[13] In this way, a new ecumenical council seemed possible, so the new assembly had its place in Nicaea between September 24 and October 13, 786. Despite the support that Irene had in the military officials, members of the tagmata (troops stationed in Constantinople) continued to be loyal to iconoclastic policy and rioted outside the council, forcing it to disband. Irene forced them to be transferred to Asia Minor, and as soon as they were outside

11. Brown, "A Dark-Age Crisis," 33–34.

12. Grabar, *L'iconoclasme*, 177.

13. Gregory, *A History of Byzantium*, 214.

the city, she had them dismissed and ordered the council to assemble again in 787.[14] The proceedings gathered 350 bishops and were presided by Tarasius. Two important decisions marked the work of the council: acceptance into the ecclesiastic community of iconoclasts who renounced their doctrine and destruction of all the iconoclastic writings. The restoration of icons was finally accomplished.[15]

The reawakening of the iconoclastic inclinations started with Emperor Leo V the Armenian (813–820). As Leo III, he also had an oriental background and was strategos of the Anatolic theme. Leo V appointed John the Grammarian as the leader of a committee whose task was to collect the theological material for the next iconoclastic council. In this period, the icons were defended by Patriarch Nicephorus and Theodore the Studite, whose opposition, however, was not strong enough to defeat the Emperor's force. On Easter 815, since Nicephorus refused to sign the iconoclastic argument made by Grammarian's commission, he was dethroned and replaced with Theodotos Melissenos, a courtier coming from one of the most prestigious aristocratic families. Under the presidency of the new Patriarch, a new council was held and confirmed the decisions of the 754 council. The council ordered the destruction of icons, but added no new arguments to the iconoclastic doctrine. The new iconoclastic impetus lacked the force characteristic of the iconoclasm of Leo III and Constantine V—it was not a renovated iconoclasm, but a weak reactionary attempt.[16] During the reign of Leo V, the persecution of images and their worshipers was very severe, but on the other hand, even the most vehement opponents of Leo V acknowledge that he was very efficient and skilful in defending the empire and wise in his administrative measures.[17]

Five years later, in the Hagia Sophia, the church in which the council of 815 was held, Leo V was assassinated by supporters of Michael II, founder of the Amorian Dynasty. Michael II did not accept the council of Nicaea nor did he approve the iconoclastic councils. Instead, his decision was to prohibit every discussion on icons. The Emperor was from Phrygia, which once was one of the centers of the iconoclastic party, so

14. Ibid.

15. Ostrogorski, *Istorija Vizantije*, 185.

16. Ibid, 206.

17. Vasiliev, *History of the Byzantine Empire*, 285.

the new ruler was undoubtedly against the cult of images, but was also aware of the unstoppable decline of the iconoclastic movement.

The iconoclasm had its final period during the reign of Theophilus (829–842), who had been crowned co-emperor in 821. Unlike his father, Theophilus was learned and cultured, having been taught by John the Grammarian. However, his military potentials were weak, and his rule was marked by the fall of Amorion (an important Byzantine city in Asia Minor and ancestral city of the Dynasty) in 838 and of entire western Sicily in 841.[18] In 837, the Grammarian became Patriarch of Constantinople and new persecutions started, just like in the epoch of Constantine V, directed primarily against the monastic circles. However, despite the force with which the Emperor and Patriarch tried to re-establish iconoclasm, the movement was weaker than ever—the iconoclastic policy found no support even in Asia Minor and survived only in the capital, thanks to the will of the Emperor and his followers.[19] When Theophilus died in 842, the iconoclastic movement also reached its end.

To judge by documents referring to the removal of religious images, it seems that the image of Christ above the Chalke Gate played the crucial role in testifying the current imperial policy. However, another example of evidence of the changing in the policy of images is very interesting—the church of the Dormition in Nicaea, originally the monastery of Hyakinthos. It was destroyed in 1922, but old photographs reveal its story. The church had an apse mosaic, whose main element was a standing Theotokos and Child. Around this representation can be seen an irregular black line on the gold background, following the outline of Mary, and cutting across the jewelled step on which she stands. Level with her elbows can be traced a further black line, extending to either side in the rough shape of a cross. The black lines on the mosaic marked irregularities of the surface on which dust and dirt had collected. They were the sutures between different phases of activity, where the old plaster had been cut and new mosaic tesserae on fresh plaster inserted. They show that the Theotokos and Child was from the final phase. This composition must have been a replacement for a large cross. However, the cross itself was a replacement for the original scheme—this too must have been a

Mother and Child, of which the inscription and most of the jewelled step had been preserved through all the other changes. To either side in the presbytery vault were pairs of angels, and these too had been removed and then replaced.[20]

## CAUSES

A lot has been said about the iconoclastic crisis in Byzantium and many scholars have dedicated themselves to the study of its history. However, it seems that there is no agreement regarding the real origins of the controversy or the causes that provoked it. This could be explained with the fact that, given its multidimensionality, the problem has been studied from various points of view—historical, ecclesiastical, theological, artistic, and each of these approaches produced its own interpretative key. For example, theologians were concerned with the Christological dimension, while historians tended to accentuate the importance of the historical events and socio-political relations in Byzantium. And, as usually happens when one tries to resolve such a complex problem, the solution stands in the analysis of all of its strata.

One of the hypotheses on the origin of the iconoclastic doctrine, also proposed in the iconophile writings, is that it was inspired by the iconoclastic tendencies of Judaism and Islam. In a letter of Patriarch Germanos addressed to Thomas of Claudiopolis, one of the iconoclastic bishops in Asia, written around 724, we read that

> we [Christians] ought to achieve the overthrow of the word and deeds gathered together by the infidels in order to inure the Church of Christ, and we should demonstrate her venerable and divine imperturbability. One thing therefore is to be understood first of all, namely, that not only just now but often the Jews too reproached us for such things [veneration of images], and that they, though being true worshipers of idols, but attempt to abuse our pure and divine faith and are eager to prevent us from our devotion for things made by human hands.[21]

---

20. Lowden, *Early Christian and Byzantine Art*, 157–58.
21. Mansi XIII:109B.

Later on, Germanus says that Saracens too have similar tendencies, but they can easily be confuted, since they venerate Kaaba and believe in various superstitions. In his letter, Germanus also warns against the danger of doubting the infallibility of the Church, provoked by an eventual rejection of images—enemies of the Cross could then accuse the Church of practicing idolatry for centuries.[22]

Another important document is a report on origins of iconoclasm, read by Presbyter John at the Council of Nicaea. In the report, it is said that a Jewish sorcerer, named Τεσσαρακοντάπηχυς (Forty Cubits), convinced the caliph Yazid II (720–724) to destroy all images. The "reward" would have been a long and successful reign of the caliph. Yazid agreed and so Christian churches were deprived of every decoration. According to the proceedings of Nicaea, this happened before the eruption of the iconoclasm in the Byzantine Empire, and Constantine of Nicolia, another follower of the iconoclastic policy, was accused of imitating the Jews and the Arabs in their crimes against churches.[23]

Precisely these two aforementioned bishops, Thomas of Claudiopolis and Constantine of Nicolia, were the ones who visited the Emperor Leo III and probably convinced him to start the iconoclastic policy.[24] It seems that Leo III believed that God was displeased with the Byzantines. It is also possible that since Muslims had chosen to eschew images in their mosques, and were extraordinarily successful in battle, it was thought that God might be punishing the Byzantines for misusing religious images and falling into idolatry. Therefore, the solution for Leo III appeared simple: to ban the religious images and hope for divine approval, which would lead to political and military success. Leo's long reign of twenty-five years could have been thus interpreted as an indication of God's satisfaction with iconoclasm.[25]

But we could ask, why would Leo III—who fought against Islam with great tenacity and since 722 forced Jews to accept the baptism—have been so inclined to adopt their religious habits? Therefore, the hypotheses on the imitation of the Judaic-Muslim tradition would be false. On the other hand, the Byzantine Empire constantly confronted Islam, both militarily

22. Mansi XIII:124D–E.
23. Mansi XIII:197ff.
24. See above n. 4.
25. Lowden, *Early Christian and Byzantine Art*, 155.

and ideologically. In the field of religion, Islam claimed to be the last, and therefore the highest and purest, revelation of God—in this context, there were frequent accusations of idolatry and polytheism against the trinitarian doctrine and the use of icons. Maybe this was the ambit in which the Emperor felt compelled to respond, purifying Christianity to better prepare it to challenge Islam.[26]

These facts are beyond doubt: the iconoclastic movement had its origins in the imperial policy and its main promoters were emperors. Iconoclasm was "an imperial heresy . . . born 'of the purple,' in the imperial palace."[27]

The existence of the Church as the community of incarnated Christ and Christians and the existence of religious art that represents Christ and his saints are two connected facts, obviously not recognized by Jews and Mohammedans, who do not believe in the Incarnation. The Jewish-Muslim iconoclasm could have, thence, appealed to the emperors, since it gave less importance to the religious part of man, who, given the Incarnation, was a being gifted with free will—a principle that contradicted any unlimited power of the government. The Byzantine emperors certainly believed in Incarnation, but they did not accept two important consequences: the absolute supremacy of the Church in spiritual affairs and the terrestrial representation of the celestial world in Christian art. This was an attack against the Church, and although they believed in the supreme and supernatural kingdom of Christ, they did not wish to permit on this earth any image but their own of their own imperial natural world. Their sacred empire had to be the only material form of the Christianity on earth, while the Church had to have just a liturgical role in the empire. Consequently, the supernatural had to remain abstract, and Christ and His celestial world was not to be expressed in visible images.[28]

The iconoclastic crisis did not, however, have consequences only for the external position of the Byzantine emperor (e.g., military campaigns, foreign policy, confrontation with Islam), but also had profound internal repercussions. One such repercussion was, as we have seen, the cruel persecution of monks. Why exactly monks were spokesmen of the

26. Meyendorff, *Byzantine Theology*, 43.

27. Gero, *Byzantine Iconoclasm*, 131.

28. Ladner, "Origin and Significance of the Byzantine Iconoclastic Controversy," in *Images and Ideas in the Middle Ages*, 47–48.

"orthodox" doctrine and why did the emperors consider such a merciless fight against them necessary?

For centuries, Byzantine monks occupied an eminent place in Byzantine society. A monk was a holy man; he was in continuous communication with God, and in the eyes of the faithful, he was one of the links between them and God. The psychological need and the emotional state of a believer were identical in front of an icon and in front of a monk. Both icon and monk were signs of the holiness on earth, and both represented "the image of God." A monk was a model and exhibited a kind of "private piety." His relation with God was solitary, and his religion was individual. This differed from the participation of faithful in the public Eucharist in great basilicas. Therefore, personal piety was dispersed towards icons, since icons led to the intercessions of saints who dwelt in the vicinity of Christ's throne. And as Peter Brown writes

> holy men and icons were implicated on a deeper level. For both were, technically, unconsecrated objects. Not only was the holy man not ordained as a priest or a bishop: his appeal was precisely that he stood outside the vested hierarchy of the Byzantine church . . . It was the schema, and consecration by the bishop, that conferred spiritual power on the holy man . . . Icons were invested with holiness in the late sixth and seventh centuries because they still expressed the continuing needs of the ancient city; they were backed up by continued loyalty to particular cult-sites, which still boasted the physical remains of supernatural protectors; they entered circulation, also, as part of the relationship between the holy man and his large urban clientele.[29]

Icon and monk were the intercessors that were needed by the faithful; they were "indirect" paths that led to God. In this sense, the respect for monks surpassed the respect for emperors—despite all his glory, the emperor could not be so close to God as was a monk. The same thing should be said for icons—no man starts crying in front of the image of an emperor, and that is exactly what happened in front of icons. Therefore, "Iconoclasm is a centripetal reaction: it asserts the unique value of a few central symbols of the Christian community that enjoyed consecration from above against the centrifugal tendencies of unconsecrated objects."[30]

29. Brown, "A Dark-Age Crisis," 17–21.
30. Ibid., 8.

The "central symbols" would have reaffirmed the importance of the community against that private religion represented by icons and monks. On a political level, the collectivity and public piety would have reinforced the centralized state, accentuating also civic patriotism and respect for the government. The measures adopted against monks were developed to break the points of contact between the spiritual power of monks and the piety of laymen, so iconoclasm would have been an attempt to destroy the informal leadership of the Christian community.

One of the interesting hypotheses in the socio-political line of explanations is Alexander Kazhdan's emphasis on family: familial ties were greatly strengthened, the possibility of divorce was restricted, and the nuclear family had become the most substantial element of economic life. So, the support of the iconoclasts for the family, and their opposition to monasticism, would not have been merely symbolic, but it was a conflict between two different forms of social organization.[31]

All these phenomena—the confrontations with Islam, the reforms of emperors, and their hostility towards monks—could be illustrative to comprehend the historical or psychological background of the iconoclastic position, but they do not sufficiently explain why images, in particular, were the object of the attack. Naturally, the political dimensions play an important role, but not a decisive one—the iconoclastic controversy cannot be considered a mere ideological superstructure with a political or economic foundation.

Very relevant in this sense is the position of Byzantine bishops—how is it possible that such a considerable number of bishops (338) would accept the iconoclastic doctrine? It seems too simple to suggest that the only reason for their behavior was to satisfy the will of the emperor. Bishops were much more moderate than some politicians, but it looks like their opposition to icons was sincere. After all, the iconoclasts felt the need to justify their position—even Constantine V wrote theological treatises, although his reasons maybe were not theological, but rather political. As a matter of fact, the iconoclastic controversy involved some "perennial" themes, such as the incarnation for the history or the definition and interpretation of Christian worship. The dispute on images transformed into a new version of Christological debates and challenged tradition, since both

---

31. Kazhdan and Constable, *People and Power in Byzantium*, 88.

parties maintained that they were following the authority of the Fathers. John Damascene, Patriarch Nicephorus, and Theodore the Studite were true theologians, and not merely polemicists or ecclesiastical conspirators. The political dimension does not diminish at all its doctrinal aspect, since "all the doctrinal movements in the Eastern Church (and possibly, all the doctrinal and philosophic movements) were, in some sense, politically involved, and had political and social implications."[32]

## DOCTRINE

All the iconoclastic writings were destroyed, so it is only through iconodules' testimonies that we can judge them. It seems that an articulated theology of iconoclasm had not been developed before Emperor Constantine V, who wrote treatises against images.

To justify his own position, Constantine refers to the first six ecumenical councils—for him, the iconoclastic doctrine was not at all new, but represented a logical result of the Christological debates of the preceding centuries. The painter, when he depicts an image of Christ, can depict only His humanity, in which case he separates it from His divinity, or both His humanity and His divinity. In the first case, he would be a Nestorian, and in the second, he assumes that the divinity is circumscribed by humanity, which is absurd; or, the two natures could be confused, in which case he would be a Monophysite.[33] By insisting on the inseparable union between the two natures of Christ, the emperor made the distinction between them almost indiscernible. Obviously, the iconoclasts supposed that the deification of Christ's humanity would have suppressed His human character, and therefore, contradicted the Chalcedonian claim according to which each nature maintains its own mode of being. Furthermore, they did not take care of the significance of the hypostasis—being assumed by the hypostasis of the Logos, human nature does not merge with the divinity, but maintains its full identity. The iconoclasts failed to understand that in the icon, it is not a *nature* (neither divine nor human) that is represented, but the *person* of Christ, who is both God and man.

32. George Florovsky, "Origen, Eusebius and the Iconoclastic Controversy," 79.
33. Mansi XIII:252A–B, 256A–B.

Another aspect of the iconoclast position was their notion of image, which they considered identical or "consubstantial" to the prototype. According to Constantine V, the definition of an icon is quite simple: the icon is the image of a *person*.[34] As simple as it may seem, this definition contains the core of his approach: in order to fulfil the claim of being an icon, a true image, it must show this person, exactly as it is. As the emperor put it, "Every image is the copy of an original . . . In order to be a true image, it has to be consubstantial with what is depicted . . . so that the whole be safeguarded; otherwise it is not an image."[35] The consequence of this approach was that a material image could never reach this identity and would, therefore, always be inadequate. This approach obviously makes icons impossible, since it is the consubstantiality that images painted on wood lack; and not only are these unacceptable as representations of Christ, but they do not deserve to be called images.[36] The only "true" image of Christ that they would admit is the sacramental image of the Eucharist as the "image" and "symbol" of Christ.[37] In the Eucharist, Christ himself offered his image, which was completely permeated by his living reality, so in this line of thought, an icon, in order to be a true icon, must represent a consubstantial likeness of the original and express the real presence of the depicted.[38]

One of the problems emphasized by the iconoclasts was the relationship between matter and spirit. As a matter of fact, the veneration of images was seen as the worship of lifeless, inanimate matter, which was opposed to the real worship "in spirit and in truth." So the iconoclastic council in one of its definitions:

> If any one spend his labour in setting up the figures of Saints in lifeless and deaf images made of material colours which cannot do

34. Nicephorus, *Scripta adversus Iconomachos* 297A.

35. Nicephorus, *Scripta adversus Iconomachos* 225A, 228D.

36. Here stands a curiosity of the iconoclastic doctrine of the image—despite the iconoclastic bishops clearly agreed with emperor's opinions, their council did not adopt his definition of the image. As a matter of fact, the iconoclastic council did not give a definition of the image at all. It is possible that the bishops tried to hide the discussion of the person of Christ, and thus prevent an iconophile response to such doctrine. What they did insist on was the impossibility to circumscribe the flesh of Christ that is totally intermingled with the divinity and thus made divine.

37. See Meyendorff, *Byzantine Theology*, 44.

38. Schönborn, *God's Human Face*, 159.

any good (for the devising of them is vain and an invention of dev-
ilish craft), and hath no care to represent in himself their virtues
as be finds them on record in the Scriptures—and so make living
images of them, as being thereby excited to zeal similar to theirs,
even as our inspired fathers have said—let him be anathema.[39]

The divinity could not be put in unworthy matter made by human
hands. It is clear here that the main distinction was between a living and a
lifeless image—this was the criterion that separated a true image from the
idol, and as already said, a true image was one that completely reproduced
the original.[40]

The principal authority of iconoclasts was the appeal to antiquity,
which was probably the strongest point of both their attack and defense.[41]
They insisted that the veneration of the falsely named images did not come
from the tradition of Christ, the apostles, or the Fathers. With the iconophile veneration of icons, they contrasted the veneration of the cross, for
which they asserted was the most ancient tradition of the Church. And
the cross was a pure symbol; it did not depict anything, just reminded of
something.

In addition to this, iconoclasts also had a heterodox vision of the
Virgin and saints. According to the report of Nicephorus, Constantine
negated the title "Theotokos" to the Virgin and "intended to completely
remove it from the liturgy of Christians."[42] It seems that he had also negated the power of the Virgin to intercede for the Church; much less efficient would be, then, the intercessions of other saints. As a matter of
fact, not only the title "Theotokos," but also the title "Saint" should have
been negated. Despite this was probably an expression of private opinion
of Constantine, the others supported him in his opposition to the cult of
the Virgin and other saints. Mary was, for most iconoclasts, the same as
she was for the orthodox: the super-glorious Mother of God. But, after all,
she was just a human being, just like the apostles, the prophets, and the
saints.[43] One thing would be the respect (τιμή) for the saints, and com-

39. Mansi XIII:345CD.
40. See Schönborn, *God's Human Face*, 152.
41. Florovsky, "Origen, Eusebius," 81.
42. Nicephorus, *Scripta adversus Iconomachos* 341.
43. Jaroslav Pelikan, *The Spirit of Eastern Christendom*, 111–12.

pletely another would be the veneration (προσκύνησις) of them and the production of their images.[44]

The situation was even more difficult for angels—at least the saints were once alive, had human faces, and were material, but angels were spirits that could not be touched and therefore could not be circumscribed in the images.

---

44. Theodorus, *Antirheticus II* 369.

# 3

## Dionysius and Images

In Gervase Mathew's words, "Much that was most vital in Byzantine art came into being through the effort to apprehend and to convey a hidden meaning."[1] The purpose was not only to grasp the beauty experienced by the senses, but the Beauty apprehended through the senses by the Mind.[2] With the latter, Dionysius was also concerned.

Two principal concepts of Dionysius' thought are, as said in ch. 1, the absolute transcendence of the divinity and the hierarchical order of the cosmos. The problem that can be foretold in this context is, how can these two fundamental concepts be conciliated? Dionysius was aware of this problem and of the difficulties that had to accompany the solution. The way out consists in the doctrine of symbol, which could offer a mode of overcoming the contrast between the divine transcendence and hierarchies. Of essential importance would then be one of Dionysius' works which he himself mentions—*The Symbolic Theology*. This, unfortunately, went missing, or maybe was never written.

*The Divine Names* closes with the words: "So here I finish my treatise on the conceptual names of God, and, with God's guidance, I will move on to *The Symbolic Theology*."[3] In the ninth letter, Dionysius informs Titus that he is sending him "the full text of my *Symbolic Theology*."[4] Obviously, Dionysius gave much importance to theological symbolism, and he probably felt the need to write a treatise on the subject—whether this treatise

---

1. Mathew, *Byzantine Aesthetics*, 39.
2. Ibid.
3. Dionysius, *De divinis nominibus* 984A.
4. Dionysius, *Epistolae* 1113B.

was actually written, we do not know. Among the writings that came to us, there is no systematic or detailed elaboration of the symbolic doctrine and, therefore, we will have to satisfy ourselves with the fragments found in the known works.

First, we must note that the Dionysian notion of σύμβολον does not fully correspond to the word "symbol." The Greek word, used by Dionysius, differs from the modern word both in meaning and in emotional connotation. In the thought of Dionysius, the word does not negate the difference between the symbol and the symbolized, but it rather represents what they have in common—symbol is not just a sign, but the very thing. Symbol is in Dionysius a most general philosophico-religious category that includes image, sign, representation, beauty, as well as many real-life objects, and, above all, the cult practice as its concrete manifestations.[5]

In the context of the Areopagite's theology, the function of the symbol stands in overcoming the contrast between God's transcendence and the hierarchy that connects God with the material world. The gnoseological basis of Dionysius' theory of symbol and image is the idea that within the hierarchical system of transmission of the information from God to man, it was necessary to qualitatively transform the information itself on the relation "heaven-earth." This is where the substantial change of the informational vehicle happens, which from spiritual converts into material.[6] This task is realized through a twofold movement—the descent, motivated by grace, of God towards humanity, and the ascent of the humanity towards God.

The revelation of the divine is not something that is strange to God, but rather follows from His nature. Despite the revelation, God does not annihilate the difference between the divine and the earthly, and in order to explain the possibility of the revelation, Dionysius uses a concept of the aesthetic thought, the one of similarity. In order for something to reveal God and to be the body of the revelation, it must, in some way, be similar to God; on the other hand, God is different from everything that we know and experience. The concept of similarity, based on the cataphatic mode of designation, is in the ambit of classical aesthetics and consists of making spiritual essences according to a "more appropriate and related fash-

5. Bychkov, *L'estetica bizantina*, 145.
6. Ibid., 144.

ioning," relating to what "we would hold to be the noblest, immaterial and transcendent beings."[7] In other words, similar images have to constitute a set of properties, peculiarities, and highly positive qualities, inherent to the things and phenomena of the material world. They have to be perfect in all aspects and representable (i.e., in words and colors)—ideal targets of the possible perfection of the material world. In the similar images, all the visible beauties of the world are concentrated.[8] However, as we said, God is different from all our knowledge and experience. Similar images are far from being similar to the divinity, for it is "far beyond every manifestation of being and of life; no reference to life can characterize it; every reason or intelligence fall short of similarity to it."[9] In respect to the first cause, the visible beauties are "base images."[10]

The way in which Dionysius resolves the dilemma is the introduction into the doctrine of the dissimilar similarity, which relates to the apophatic designations of the divinity:

> But surely there is no need to dwell on this point, for scripture itself asserts that God is dissimilar and that he is not to be compared with anything, that he is different from everything and, stranger yet, that there is none at all like him. Nevertheless words of this sort do not contradict the similarity of things to him, for the very same things are both similar and dissimilar to God. They are similar to him to the extent that they share what cannot be shared. They are dissimilar to him in that as effects they fall so very far short of their Cause and are infinitely and incomparably subordinate to him.[11]

The use of the concept of similarity, but also of imitation, show an aesthetic implication of Dionysius' thought—the dissimilar similarity epitomizes his tendency to perceive contrasts as the proper structure of reality. The way in which the divinity reveals itself to our eyes is not a simple optical illusion, a deception of our senses. The similarity denotes a property of what really exists and it is not simply an impression of the spectator. A thing can be similar to another because it participates in its

7. Dionysius, *De coelesti hierarchia* 137C.

8. Bychkov, *L'estetica bizantina*, 154.

9. Dionysius, *De coelesti hierarchia* 140C.

10. Dionysius, *De coelesti hierarchia* 141B.

11. Dionysius, *De divinis nominibus* 916A.

nature—the more one thing participates in another, the more similar it will be to it. However, in the context of the revelation, the similarity can never be complete, since then the divine transcendence would be annihilated.[12]

Concepts like similarity, imitation, symbol, etc., imply the capacity to perceive sensible objects—it is through these objects that we know God: "God is therefore known in all things and as distinct from all things. He is known through knowledge and through unknowing. Of him there is conception, reason, understanding, *touch*, *perception*, opinion, *imagination*, name, and many other things."[13] Since every being is from God, then we might say that He is known in every "touch" and in every sensation, i.e., the Cause is touched and sensed in Its effects and through Its effects. Human beings know through senses. The human mind, moving from effects to causes, is capable of reaching a partial, but real, knowledge that the "divine Wisdom is the source, the cause, the substance, the perfection, the protector, and the goal."[14] Our senses are like "an echo of the wisdom."

Dionysius will many times affirm that the capacity to receive the revelation of God differs from person to person. For the Areopagite, the one who receives the revelation and contemplates symbols is not something abstract or some pure logical requisite, but a real person with individual limitations:

> There are numerous impressions of the seal and these all have a share in the original prototype; it is the same whole seal in each of the impressions and none participates in only a part . . . Maybe someone will say that the seal is not totally identical in all the reproductions of it. My answer is that this is not because of the seal itself, which gives itself completely and identically to each. The substances which receive a share of the seal are different. Hence the impressions of the one entire identical archetype are different. If the substances are soft, easily shaped, and smooth, if no impressions have been made on them already, if they are not hard and resistant,if they are not excessively soft and melting, the imprint on them will be clear, plain, and long-lasting. But if the material is lacking in this receptivity, this would be the cause of its mistaken

12. Barasch, *Icon*, 169–70.

13. Dionysius, *De divinis nominibus* 872A.

14. Dionysius, *De divinis nominibus* 868C.

or unclear imprint or of whatever else results from the unreceptivity of its participation.[15]

The revelation of God is perceived and comprised in a variety of modes, which depend on the differences of the things called to participate—these differences are a universal human condition. Given the reality of the human person, called to receive the revelation, the divinity cannot be perceived without the help of mediators, which Dionysius calls "sacred veils." Speaking of the light and divine rays, Dionysius affirms that the divine ray "can enlighten us only by being upliftingly concealed in a variety of sacred veils which the Providence of the Father adapts to our nature as human beings."

The veils not only come from God, but they express His goodness and His love for human beings—they represent a concession to our imperfect nature and our mode of conceiving things. These veils are identified with appearances of beauty, odors, light, and Eucharist:

> Hence, any thinking person realizes that the appearances of beauty are signs of an invisible loveliness. The beautiful odors which strike the senses are representations of a conceptual diffusion. Material lights are images of the outpouring of an immaterial gift of light. The thoroughness of sacred discipleship indicates the immense contemplative capacity of the mind. Order and rank here below are a sign of the harmonious ordering toward the divine realm. The reception of the most divine Eucharist is a symbol of participation in Jesus. And so it goes for all the gifts transcendently received by the beings of heaven, gifts which are granted to us in a symbolic mode.[16]

If theology uses poetic language, it does so only to open the path that would be accessible to our imperfect nature. Therefore, images and poetic representations were not made out of artistic interest, but they are signs of God's intention to facilitate our perception of the revelation. The veils of which Dionysius speaks not only attenuate the light that irradiates from the divine principle, making it perceptible to human eyes, but they also have an active role—they incite humans to go beyond the mere exterior perception.[17] As a matter of fact, there are two types of symbols

---

15. Dionysius, *De divinis nominibus* 644A–C.

16. Dionysius, *De coelesti hierarchia* 121D–124A.

17. Barasch, *Icon*, 175.

that designate the divinity: they can work "firstly, by proceeding naturally through sacred images in which like represents like, or also using formations which are dissimilar and even entirely inadequate and ridiculous." The first "sacred shapes" (or images) are particularly dangerous, because they can deceive humans and induce them to interpret these images literally, and here stands the danger of idolatry. That is why Dionysius prefers the second type of symbols:

> Since the way of negation appears to be more suitable to the realm of the divine and since positive affirmations are always unfitting to the hiddenness of the inexpressible, a manifestation through dissimilar shapes is more correctly to be applied to the invisible. So it is that scriptural writings, far from demeaning the ranks of heaven, actually pay them honor by describing them with dissimilar shapes so completely at variance with what they really are that we come to discover how those ranks, so far removed from us, transcend all materiality. Furthermore, I doubt that anyone would refuse to acknowledge that incongruities are more suitable for lifting our minds up into the domain of the spiritual than similarities are. High-flown shapes could well mislead someone into thinking that the heavenly beings are golden or gleaming men, glamorous, wearing lustrous clothing, giving off flames which cause no harm, or that they have other similar beauties with which the word of God has fashioned the heavenly minds. It was to avoid this kind of misunderstanding among those incapable of rising above visible beauty that the pious theologians so wisely and upliftingly stooped to incongruous dissimilarities, for by doing this they took account of our inherent tendency toward the material and our willingness to be lazily satisfied by base images. At the same time they enabled that part of the soul which longs for the things above actually to rise up. Indeed the sheer crassness of the signs is a goad so that even the materially inclined cannot accept that it could be permitted or true that the celestial and divine sights could be conveyed by such shameful things.[18]

It is necessary, therefore, to learn to interpret the dissimilar similarities and to transfer the attributes such as rage or desire from the realm of senses, the lower one, to the celestial realm, the higher one. The complete knowledge of symbols gives exquisite and incommensurable pleasure that spurts from the contemplation of the indescribable perfection and

---

18. Dionysius, *De coelesti hierarchia* 141A–C.

from the perception of the knowledge of God, i.e., it takes to the aesthetic conclusion of the cognitive process.[19]

Without such hermeneutical transfer, attributes such as ignorance would be completely inadequate to the celestial dominion and would remain an incomprehensible dissimilarity until they would incite the reader to start the interpretative process. When this type of exegetical adjustment is realized, then the attributes can be understood and become revealing.[20] With this adjustment, the Scriptures can use a variety of material symbols, bestial or even ridiculous, in order to designate celestial beings. Properly understood, even the physical matter can be related to the divine and help our ascent. Dionysius himself will give an autobiographic testimony of the significance of symbols:

> And I myself might not have been stirred from this difficulty to my current inquiry, to an uplifting through a precise explanation of these sacred truths, had I not been troubled by the deformed imagery used by scripture in regard to the angels. My mind was not permitted to dwell on imagery so inadequate, but was provoked to get behind the material show, to get accustomed to the idea of going beyond appearances to those upliftings which are not of this world.[21]

The representation of spiritual meaning of the Scriptures as understood by Dionysius proves his great ability to combine Neoplatonism and Christianity, thus reinforcing a theurgical interpretation of sacramentalism and liturgy. Theurgy in Dionysius is synonymous with the process of the reversion:

> Now the most holy hierarchy among the beings of heaven possesses the native sacramental power of a most completely immaterial conception of God and of things divine. It is their lot to be as like God and as imitative of God as is possible. These first beings around God lead others and with their light guide them toward this sacred perfection. To the sacred orders farther down the scale they generously bestow, in proportion to their capacity, the knowledge of the workings of God, knowledge forever made available as a gift to themselves by that divinity which is absolute perfec-

19. Bychkov, *L'estetica bizantina*, 147.

20. Rorem, *Pseudo-Dionysius*, 55.

21. Dionysius, *De coelesti hierarchia* 145B.

tion and which is the source of wisdom for the divinely intelligent beings. The ranks coming in succession to these premier beings are sacredly lifted up by their mediation to enlightenment in the sacred workings of the divinity. They form the orders of initiates and they are named as such.[22]

The process of reversion is initiated sacramentally and it represents the unification with and ascending return to God that enables man to become a member of the divine community.[23] In this community, the order of hierarchs "makes known the works of God by way of the sacred symbols and it prepares the postulants to contemplate and participate in the holy sacraments."[24]

As it is clear, the dissimilar images are made on opposite principles and, unlike similar images, are connected to other aspects of the gnoseo-logical function of image. They do not "reflect," but more "indicate" the truth, and to be understood they need a rationalistic explanation. Since the truth is transcendent, it can be grasped only through its antithesis with allusions and deceptions. In order for these "types for the typeless" to reveal the information they contain, they need an adequate decryption, the theological explanation, since, according to the Byzantine tradition, a true theologian explains divine signs and symbols not according to his own judgment, but by "the power granted by the Spirit"[25], which gives him the interpretative key.[26]

Dionysius' goal here is to help the reader to get used to going beyond appearances in order to be able to recognize and comprehend any type of symbol. The pedagogical preference for dissimilar symbols is clear—ab-surdities are not immediately accepted and require an explanation. When beginners get used to this, they can pass to less astonishing symbols, without falling in danger of interpreting them literally. However, symbols not only have a revealing role, but they also serve to conceal. Their role is to keep away the unlearned from the highest and most true knowledge:

22. Dionysius, *De ecclesiastica hierarchia* 501A–B.
23. Kharlamov, *The Beauty of the Unity*, 138.
24. Dionysius, *De ecclesiastica hierarchia* 505D.
25. Dionysius, *De ecclesiastica hierarchia* 585B.
26. Bychkov, *Ľestetica bizantina*, 158.

But if one looks at the truth of the matter, the sacred wisdom of scripture becomes evident, for, when the heavenly intelligences are represented with forms, great providential care is taken to offer no insult to the divine powers, as one might say, and we ourselves are spared a passionate dependence upon images which have something of the lowly and the vulgar about them. Now there are two reasons for creating types for the typeless, for giving shape to what is actually without shape. First, we lack the ability to be directly raised up to conceptual contemplations. We need our own upliftings that come naturally to us and which can raise before us the permitted forms of the marvelous and unformed sights. Second, it is most fitting to the mysterious passages of scripture that the sacred and hidden truth about the celestial intelligences be concealed through the inexpressible and the sacred and be inaccessible to the *hoi polloi*. Not everyone is sacred, and, as scripture says, knowledge is not for everyone.[27]

The final goal of the ascent and movement through symbols is the cloud of unknowing and the apophatic theology. The result of the ascent is, therefore, the negation, the cloud of unknowing, the deprivation of sight, and, hence, the negation of the visible form. In the metaphor on the sculptor who detaches every obstacle from the vision of the hidden image, this work does not lead to the appearance of a certain figure, but rather to a revealing of a"beauty" that does not consist of distinct forms. The transcendent divinity is identified with the simplicity, and this means that the divinity is deprived of every dissimilarity, but also of every form.[28]

Even though the final goal of the ascent is the dominion without form, this path begins with objects endowed with form. The image and the vision stimulate the mind in its flight: "So there is nothing absurd in rising up, as we do, from obscure images to the single Cause of everything, rising with eyes that see beyond the cosmos to contemplate all things."[29] Thanks to the splendor of beauty and the involvement of the emotive-psychic ambit and the sensible, besides the intellectual one, an anagogical function is being fulfilled: from the visible field it becomes possible to climb to the invisible one, from a sensible experience to a spiritual one. It becomes possible the experience of God. This is a mystical, unit-

27. Dionysius, *De coelesti hierarchia* 140A–B.

28. Barasch, *Icon*, 178.

29. Dionysius, *De divinis nominibus* 821B.

ing experience, that leaves as a consequence in man the possibility to be invested of divine grace and, hence, of salvation. The symbolic language overcomes the force of the discursive one. As we have seen, this force is potentiated by dissimilar symbols, which, instead of bringing near two worlds in similarity, bring them near in dissimilarity, according to the apophatic style. The force of the symbolic language introduces us, mystically, to the intuition of the logically contradictory truth.

Speaking of ecclesiastical hierarchs, Dionysius will say that "using images derived from the senses they spoke of the transcendent," and they do it because "in a divine fashion it needs perceptible things to lift us up into the domain of conceptions."[30] When commenting on the vision of Ezechiel, the Areopagite affirms:

> The Word of God furthermore attributes to the heavenly beings the form of bronze, of electrum, of multicolored stones, and if it does so the reason lies in the fact that electrum, which contains gold and silver, symbolizes both the incorruptible, priceless, unfailing, and unpolluted radiance of gold as well as the gleam, the gloss, the splendor, and the heavenly glow of silver. As for bronze, it recalls either fire or gold, for the reasons given. With regard to the multicolored stones, these must be taken to work symbolically as follows: white for light, red for fire, yellow for gold, green for youthful vitality. Indeed you will find that each form carries an uplifting explanation of the representational images.[31]

Images for Dionysius do not have an artistic value, or even if they have, he is not concerned with this dimension of symbols. Rather, images have a pedagogical and anagogical value. Here stands one of the paradoxes of Dionysian thought—on the one hand, the apparently improper symbols provoke wonder and induce an attempt to take off the "veil," and on the other, symbolic images, as perceptible and material objects, serve as a starting point of the human mind's ascent towards the spiritual world, towards the unknowable God. So, the dissimilar images are not only conventional signs and rationalistic symbols. Their organization is more complex. Since they also have a psychological role, they stimulate and elevate the soul. And this stimulus is not just rational and intellectual,

---

30. Dionysius, *De ecclesiastica hierarchia* 376D–377A.
31. Dionysius, *De coelesti hierarchia* 336B–C.

but also subconscious and emotional. Its goal is the elevation of the human spirit from sensible images to the truth.[32]

This gradual ascent reminds one of the Platonic scale of *eros*—for Plato too, sensible things represent the first stair of the scale, whose end is the Beauty itself, which is nothing but the Good that manifests itself. The peak of such a process is the comprehension of the One, made visible through the Beauty. In the final moment, Eros grasps the Beauty unifying himself with It in a sort of *unio mystica*.[33] A part of his Platonic inheritance would be Dionysius' claim that the more noble a being is, the more fully it manifests the Forms. The importance of sensible things, confirmed by Dionysius, had great success in the Byzantine tradition, and, even more significant for this work, it found a strong support in the doctrine of John Damascene and other defenders of icons.

In short, images for Dionysius have the role to: designate the spiritual essences; elevate man to them, and truly reveal the world of the super-being on the level of the being. This idea of image is the main modality through which the union between the levels of super-being and being can be realized. Only in the image and through it is the unknowable unity of God's transcendence and immanence possible. Speaking of the elevation of the human soul, the same thing should be said about the Byzantine notion of beauty. According to the Areopagite, the absolute beauty (or true beauty, or divine beauty) is a model, a creative cause of everything, the source of all beauty, the reason for the cosmic eurythmy, the object of love, and the goal of every aspiration and movement.[34] Byzantines, as well as Dionysius, concentrated their attention on the psychological aspect of the influence that art and the beautiful exercised on man. The psychology, which reflected connections between concrete persons and their mutable interrelations, formed an important part of Byzantine gnoseology and one of the principal nerves of entire spiritual life. The comprehension of the absolute beauty was carried out on the level of the psychic subconscious (super-sensible and super-rational) in the process of liturgical and artistic experience.[35] The conclusion that imposes itself from the consideration of the place of symbols in the Dionysian writings is that images play an

---

32. Bychkov, *L'estetica bizantina*, 158.

33. Ivanovic, "Ancient EROS and Medieval AGAPE," 103.

34. Dionysius, *De divinis nominibus* 701C–D, 704A.

35. Bychkov, *L'estetica bizantina*, 100.

eminent role in the most important process of the human soul, the ascent to God—images are the starting point of the flight to the heaven.

# 4

## The Orthodox Theology of the Icon and the Dionysian Influence

### INTRODUCTORY REMARKS

Ernst Kitzinger established that there is no evidence on the cult of images before the third century.[1] As a matter of fact, the art in the early centuries of Christianity was not art in the strict sense—visual representations were limited to sketches, signs and symbols. The paintings were rudimentary and usually with limited spectrum of colors. They represented more reminders and mementos than real images of worship.[2]

It was after Justinian's era that images acquired greater weight—references of pilgrims to the Holy Land, which contained no stories on religious images in preceding centuries, started mentioning holy images in this period. Images also began to occupy a place in the profane literature and in the lives of saints and important men.

For example, an episode told in the Life of Saint Maximus the Confessor recounts the dispute of Maximus with Theodosius, bishop of Caesarea, in 656, in the castrum of Byzia in Bitiny, where Maximus was imprisoned. At a certain moment of the dispute, when an agreement seemed to be reached, all the participants prayed, and kissed the book of Gospel, the cross, and the icon of Christ and the Virgin. In the end, they posed their hands on these objects in a sense of confirmation (βεβάωσις)

1. Kitzinger, "The Cult Of Images," 86.
2. Besançon, *The Forbidden Image*, 110.

of the agreement.[3] In a text contained in an anonymous Syriac compilation composed in 569, a story tells that in the years from 554 to 560 a copy of the miraculous images of Christ had been taken by priests in solemn procession through various cities of Asia Minor, with the scope to collect financial contributions for a church in a village destroyed by barbarians. The text tells that the image of Christ received the same respect as the image of the Emperor.[4]

The image not only became the object of devotion, but it was also attributed magical powers. The most famous story on this aspect of icons is the one on the image of Christ in Edessa, told by Evagrius in his *Ecclesiastical History*. The tradition says that Christ sent his image to King Agbar, prince of Osroene, king of Edessa. The Orthodox Church celebrates the translation of the image of Edessa on August 16, and a sticheron from the eight tone of vespers says: "Having represented your very pure face, / You sent it to the faithful Agbar who had wanted to see you, / You who, in keeping with Thy Divinity, are invisible to the Cherubim."[5] According to the story, the image had a decisive role in the battle against the Persians—the miraculous intercession of the icon was to be the materialized proof of the ancient belief that Edessa had special protection of Christ. If the attack of Persians were considered an attempt of the infidels to challenge Christ's power, then, for the believers, it would be natural to ascribe the victory to the divine intervention.[6] At any rate, this story contributed greatly to the distribution of the cult of images and accentuated the attribution of magical powers to images.

The story of the image of Edessa goes side by side with the use of icons in private homes, in which they were to have a protective role. This private cult of images gradually transformed into a public cult. As a matter of fact, the same story of Edessa shows this gradual transformation—the operation with which the magical power of image was realized took place in secret in an underground passage.

The sacred images gradually acquired the form of *palladium*, which is the object of a public cult and has the scope to encourage its possessors and intimidate their enemies. In successive versions of the event in

3. PG 90:156A–B, 164A–B.

4. Kitzinger, "The Cult of Images," 99–100.

5. Besançon, *The Forbidden Image*, 111.

6. Cited in Kitzinger, "The Cult of Images," 103.

Edessa, the image of Christ underwent precisely this transformation—from *apotropaion* it became *palladium*.[7] *Palladii* found their places in Alexandria, Caesarea, and Antioch. Furthermore, they played an important role during military campaigns, such as during the war of Emperor Heraclius against the Persians.[8]

A considerable number of icons found in the hagiographic literature of the post-Justinian era are described not as belonging to churches or private houses, but as situated in public places, particularly near the gates of cities, where they fulfilled an apotropaic role, comparable to the role of the image of Edessa. The most memorable story of this kind is the role of images in the defense of Constantinople in 626: the Patriarch ordered depiction of images of the Virgin and Christ on the western gates of the city, which helped the defenders to resist the attack of Avars.

It seems evident that the icon was preceded by icons and that it accompanied sacred images in future periods. When the cult of images began to spread, usually it had to do with an object which, given its true or alleged origin, was associated with the relic and participated in its nature. Most initial news on the adoration or other kind of ceremonial veneration concerned the ἀχειροποίητοι, which were assumed to be produced by direct contact with the divinity, or images which, although created by human hands, were physically associated to sacred relics, or, in the end, images made or blessed by a living saint, e. g., a stylite.[9]

On the other hand, one should not search for an association with relics in every kind of cult of images. The respect for images and visual representations was rooted in the Greek mentality all the way back to its pagan origins. The image possessed a strong suggestive power to which the Greeks and the Hellenized Semites were particularly susceptible.

---

7. Kitzinger, "The Cult of Images," 110.

8. Heraclius probably used the image of Camuliana, which represents an ἀχειροποίητος (the image made not by hands of a painter, but coming from heaven—as a Syriac chronicle of 569 tells, a woman who wished to personally see the face of Christ, found the image in the lake of her garden).

9. Kitzinger, "The Cult of Images," 116–17.

## THE DEFENSE OF IMAGES

In the pagan inheritance of the Christian Church, one should look for the roots of doctrinal accusations that the iconoclasts directed against iconodules. In fact, the primary accusation, at least in the beginning of the controversy, was the idolatry. The source of such accusation is the second commandment in Exodus of the Old Testament: "Thou shalt not make unto thee a graven image, nor any manner of likeness, of any thing that is in heaven above, or that is in the earth beneath, or that is in the water under the earth; thou shalt not bow down unto them, nor serve them." According to the iconoclast conception, it is impossible to represent man-God: "No man hath beheld God at any time" (1 John 4:12). The iconoclasts, therefore, refer above all to the Old Testament's prohibition, so images of God would, for them, be nothing but idols.

The root of the veneration of icons is the conception that material objects can be the collocation of the divine power and that this power can be assured through contact with the sacred object. This is a conception shared by both iconoclasts and iconodules—it is the foundation of the universal belief of Eastern Christians on sacraments or "mysteries." For iconoclasts, the sacrament of the Eucharist was the only admissible image of God: "The bread that we receive is an image of His [Christ's] body, which takes the form of His flesh and becomes a type of His body." On the other hand, the defenders of images affirmed that the real presence of Christ's body in the Eucharist is itself the reality, the very truth itself.

Both iconoclasts and iconodules called the elements of the liturgy "true present signs of body and blood of Christ." Iconodules admitted that the iconoclasts truly taught the real presence of body and blood of Christ in the Eucharist, but they also sustained that this was not true in the rest of their theology. The question regarding the Eucharist was not primarily the nature of the Eucharistic presence, but its implications for the definition of the "image" and for the use of images.[10] In fact, the query could be posed as follows: Can the Eucharistic presence be extended to a general principle of the sacramental mediation of the divine power through material objects, or is it an exclusive principle that does not preclude a similar extension to other means of grace, i.e., to images?

10. Pelikan, *The Spirit of Eastern Christendom*, 94.

The iconoclasts saw in the Eucharist the only adequate image of Christ, because it was consubstantial to Him, ὁμοούσιος, identical, ταυτό, according to nature, κατ'οὐσίαν. Now, the Eucharist is a miracle in which the cosmic matter (bread and wine) is being transmuted into celestial matter of the transfigured body of Christ, but this miracle is verified without any similarity. Every vision of the "flesh" in the chalice is severely forbidden by canons, and every "apparition" of this kind is considered a temptation against nature. The Verb "hypostatizes," appropriates the Eucharistic elements, integrates them into its spiritual body, but this substantial identity hides the Eucharistic presence of Christ, not just under the veil inherent to every mystery, but because this presence, not being visible, is without image. The visible (bread) is simply affirmed as identical to the invisible (the celestial body), but the operation leaves no place to the vision. The Eucharist cannot in any way serve as icon because it is only the Supper of the Lord that has to be consumed and not contemplated.[11]

The icon excludes every identification and underlines the difference of nature between the image and its prototype, between the representation and that which is represented. This difference between image and its prototype will be the basis of the defense of icons. Sacred images permit a communion of prayer, which is not the Eucharistic substantial communion with the glorified nature of Christ, but is a mystical, spiritual communion with His Person.[12]

The reverence for images was already profoundly collocated in the spiritual mentality of believers in the Orient and was passionately defended by John Damascene, Theodore the Studite, and Nicephorus of Constantinople, thanks to whom the doctrine of the icon was definitely formulated.

The *Three Treatises on the Divine Images*, written by John Damascene, are the first attempts of a Christian theologian to formulate a coherent theory of images. Damascene's discourses, in fact, respond to simple questions, such as, "What is an image?," "What type of images are there and what are they?" The theory of images, on the other hand, has a long and rich history, which begins in antiquity. Damascene, however, did not

11. Evdokimov, *Teologia della bellezza*, 195.
12. Ibid.

try to be original or to import innovations—his discourses are provoked by a controversy and serve to expose scriptural and patristic doctrines, and to provide an efficient way to defend icons.[13]

In his theory of images, John distinguishes between images according to nature (κατά φύσιν) and images according to imitation, or art (μίμησις). In the hierarchical order, images according to nature are put in the first place, and images according to imitation occupy the second. The first class of images is, according to John, "the natural image," a term that denotes a primordial relation, considered as a primary and irreducible component of a supreme reality. This general affirmation becomes particularly valid if it refers to the Son as the live, substantial, immutable, and natural image[14] of the Father who is the cause and principle of the other two persons and the principle of the relations from which the hypostases receive their distinct characteristics.

The second type of images "is the conception there is in God of what he is going to bring about, that is his pre-eternal will, which eternally holds sway in like manner."[15] This concept explains how God created the world and implicitly exemplifies that things not yet created pre-exist in the divine mind as ideas, i.e., paradigms. Images and models of things produced by God are the thought of each of them, which are also said to be predeterminations (or predefinitions). Damascene relays here directly on Dionysius, who writes in *The Divine Names*,

> We give the name of "exemplar" to those principles which preexist as a unity in God and which produce the essences of things. Theology calls them predefining, divine and good acts of will which determine and create things and in accordance with which the Transcendent One predefined and brought into being everything that is.[16]

Man, as the image of God, is the third type of image. This type regards a potential relation of assimilation and imitation according to grace of the Holy Spirit, in which the substances of image and model remain distinct.

13. Barasch, *Icon*, 188.

14. *Oratio* I:9; III:15.

15. *Oratio* III:19.

16. Dionysius *De divinis nominibus* 824C.

The fourth type of images is the most complex, and it includes images of invisible things. Here too John is in full agreement with Dionysius:

> Then again there are images of invisible and formless things, that provide in bodily form a dim understanding of what is depicted. For Scripture applies forms to God and the angels, and the same divine man [Dionysius] gives the reason when he says that if forms for formless things and shapes for shapeless things are proposed, someone might say that not the least reason is because our analogies are not capable of raising us immediately to intellectual contemplation but need familiar and natural points of reference.[17]

Damascene finds as inspiration a passage from *The Celestial Hierarchy*:

> All this accounts for the fact that the sacred institution and source of perfection established our most pious hierarchy. He modeled it on the hierarchies of heaven, and clothed these immaterial hierarchies in numerous material figures and forms so that, in a way appropriate to our nature, we might be uplifted from these most venerable images to interpretations and assimilations which are simple and inexpressible. For it is quite impossible that we humans should, in any immaterial way, rise up to imitate and to contemplate the heavenly hierarchies without the aid of those material means capable of guiding us as our nature requires.[18]

Similar to the fourth type, the fifth type also exposes the idea of analogy, but limited to the specific dominion of history. This type of image represents the theological comprehension of past events and concerns the prefiguration (προεικονίζειν) of future events.

The sixth type consists of heterogeneous elements, words, material objects, and icons. This type of image is twofold—through the word written in books and through sensible visions. Examples of these images include the Law engraved by God on tablets or the order of God that the jar and the rod be placed in the ark. Under this type also fall images made by man, i.e., icons.[19]

It should be noted that John puts icons in the last place, i.e., in the last of his categories of images, a fact that could induce one to think that icons are for him less important than other images. As a matter of fact, the

17. *Oratio* I:11.

18. Dionysius *De coelesti hierarchia* 121C–D.

19. *Oratio* III:23.

categorization of images, according to Damascene, has a hierarchical and twofold character: ascending and descending, i.e., from God to creatures, and from creatures to God.[20] This order reminds one of the movements of which Dionysius speaks—the Areopagite too establishes a twofold movement, exactly as John does, from the created world to God, and from God to the created world. Precisely as symbols are, for Dionysius, the first step in the ascent to God, icons have the same role for John. In both, icon is the beginning of the movement by which creature (man) returns back to God.

The categorization of images is present also in Theodore the Studite; he, however, divides them into two groups—natural images and artificial images. The natural image has a natural relation, while the artificial one has an artificial relation. The natural image is identical in both substance and likeness to its prototype, as Christ is identical to the Father. If the artificial image had the same characteristics as natural image, then the iconoclastic argument would be valid. However, the artificial image is identical to its prototype in likeness, but it differs in substance.[21] Very similar to this is Dionysius' argument that allows visual symbols, but claims abyss between matter and "celestial substance." Artificial images for Theodore have the same meaning as material symbols for Dionysius.

For iconodule theologians it seems that each creature could be considered an image in the wide sense, since all creatures are modelled according to ideas contained in God, who is the celestial prototype.

The fundamental point of a correct theology of icon is the distinction between image and its prototype, and this is what the defenders of icons tried to prove. In fact, there is a close relation between image and its prototype, but this does not imply the identity in substance—the specific relation is the one of "similarity" and "identity of likeness," as Damascene put it. It seems that this similarity is, for John, the partial identity contained in the form of both icon and prototype.[22] According to him, the image of a man represents the almost identical likeness of his corporeal form, although it differs from it—the image is not animated, and it cannot speak, feel, think . . .[23] This, however, is not true for the natural image,

20. Strezova, "Relation of Image," 90–91.

21. Theodorus *Antirrheticus* III 392.

22. Strezova, "Relation of Image," 94.

23. *Oratio* III:16.

since Christ is the living substantial image of the Father and differs from the Father only in the hypostatic properties. From this claim it follows that the icon resembles the prototype only in the visible form, and not in essence. Nevertheless, the material image participates to a certain extent in the prototype—it concerns representation and partaking of identity and name. Every confusion of substance is, however, rejected, since this type of relational participation is not equal to the hypostatic union.

According to John, the sanctity is expressed in icons through their prototypes, and therefore, icons too become sanctified. At this point, Damascene's doctrine also leans on the conceptions of the Areopagite. In *The Ecclesiastical Hierarchy*, speaking of sacraments, Dionysius writes, "It is while there are placed on the divine altar the reverend symbols by which Christ is signaled and partaken that one immediately reads out the names of the saints."[24] The sacrament, therefore, participates in the nature of Christ. In the same work, Dionysius considers the funeral rites and explains that the divine communion is given to both soul and body: "And they do so for the body by way of the imagery of the most divine ointment and through the most sacred symbol of the divine communion."[25] Again, it is clear that the symbol of Christ is not just a sign, but it takes part in the nature of Christ and, hence, communicates sanctity.

The difference between image and prototype means that the religious contents, the mystical essence of the icon relates only to the hypostatic presence. Therefore, there is not any ontology inscribed in the nature of icon. It does not contain any nature, it does not attract or retain anything, but the Name-Hypostasis irradiates in it, beyond every imprisonment in the volume itself of the table. Icon has no proper existence; being participation and "leading image," it leads to the prototype, announces its presence, and testifies its parousia. The icon, the material point of this world, opens a gap—the Transcendent breaks into it, and the successive waves of Its presence transcend every limit and fill in the universe.[26]

One of the most important functions of the icon is its educative role. As Kitzinger notes, "The defense of the visual arts, initiated by the Cappadocian Fathers in the second half of the fourth century, was based on their usefulness as educational tools. Imagery was γραφὴ σιωπῶσα, a

24. Dionysius *De ecclesiastica hierarchia* 437C.

25. Dionysius *De ecclesiastica hierarchia* 565B.

26. Evdokimov, *Teologia della bellezza*, 196–97.

means of instruction or edification, especially for the illiterate. The stress may be either on intellectual nourishment or on moral education."[27] The conception of the icon as an educational instrument useful for the communication with the divine found its place also in the doctrine of John: "What the book does for those who understand letters, the image does for the illiterate."[28] And again:

> Every image makes manifest and demonstrates something hidden. For example, because human beings do not have direct knowledge of what is invisible, since their souls are veiled by bodies, or [knowledge] if future events, or of things distant and removed in space, since they are circumscribed by space and time, the image was devised to guide us to knowledge and to make manifest and open what is hidden, certainly for our profit and well-doing and salvation, so that, as we learn what is hidden from things recorded and noised abroad, we are filled with desire and zeal for what is good, and avoid and hate the opposite, that is, what is evil.[29]

Precisely the same scope Dionysius has in mind when he speaks of "material instruments capable of guiding us,"[30] as well as when he explains that God revealed the angelic hierarchy to us "in the sacred pictures of the scriptures so that he might lift us in spirit up through the perceptible to the conceptual, from sacred shapes and symbols to the simple peaks of the hierarchies of heaven."[31]

In close with the educational role of the icon stands its "psychological" influence. Writing in the first half of the seventh century, Leontius of Neapolis asked his readers if one would not want to kiss the clothes of his deceased wife in order to maintain the memory of her, and claimed that Christian icons are not but especially vivid examples of such memory. In a similar way, Damascene notes, "Many times I have seen those who long for someone, when they have seen his garment, greet it with their eyes and lips, as if it were the one longed for himself."[32] The Christian veneration of icons was an example of this kind of devotion, in which respect

---

27. Kitzinger, "The Cult of Images," 136.

28. *Oratio* I:17.

29. *Oratio* III:17.

30. Dionysius, *De coelesti hierarchia* 121D.

31. Dionysius, *De coelesti hierarchia* 124A.

32. *Oratio* III:10.

and affection were given to the garment, but were, in fact, directed to the person passed away—Christ, His mother, or a saint. It is in this sense that he saw the image as a mirror suitable for the obtuseness of man's physical constitution. Since this was the condition of humanity, the use of similar instruments was somewhat appropriate.

One of the characteristics of such psychology, particularly revealing for Christian images, was the role of sight. For Damascene, who quotes the words of the Lord—"Blessed are your eyes, for they see, and your ears, for they hear" (Matt 13:16)—Christ gave His approval to the research of beauty through sight, and hence to the use of icons as a modern substitute for miracles and other acts that His disciples were privileged to behold.[33] When the prophet Isaiah, in his inaugural vision, saw the Lord at His throne in the temple, this was the proof of the precedence of sight with respect to hearing "according to its local position and according to its sensible perception."[34] As the announcement of the Gospel was communicated through words of those who had seen the events there described, icons can be appropriate for the same scope. The sight was consecrated through the visible appearance of God in Christ, just as hearing was consecrated through the word of God. Icon served as the instrument for this consecration of sight, combined with the hearing of the word.[35]

The main source of the accusation against the iconodules was the Old Testament and its prohibition of the idolatrous practice. An idol was a representation of persons or things deprived of reality or substance, while an icon represented real persons—those who could not comprehend this distinction had to be accused of idolatry. Images of pagan veneration were put in devil's service, but icons of Christian veneration were dedicated to the glory of the true God. The representation of Christ in icons was a way to dissipate the idolatry, and not to restore it. By ascribing to the icon of Christ those Old Testament's commandments against the idolatrous representations of Greeks, iconoclasts misinterpreted the intention of the Scriptures. As a matter of fact, God himself was the first to make images of himself—the eternal Son of God as "the image of invisible God" and then Adam, made in the image of God:

33. *Oratio* III:12.

34. Theodorus *Antirrheticus* III 392.

35. Pelikan, *The Spirit of Eastern Christendom*, 121–22.

> God Himself first begat his Only-begotten Son and Word, his liv-
> ing and natural image, the exact imprint of his eternity; he then
> made human kind in accordance with the same image and like-
> ness . . . No one, however, saw the nature of God, but the figure and
> image of one who was yet to come. For the invisible Son and Word
> of God was about to become truly human, that he might be united
> to our nature and seen upon earth.[36]

The most important proof of their position, the iconoclasts found in
the Decalogue. However, the same book of Moses, which contained the
prohibition of images, contained also the description of the construction
of the tabernacle, with image of Cherubims. These images of Cherubims
could not be incorporeal, as Cherubims were, but had to be "sacred images of them," which, however, were called "Cherubims."[37] It was evident
then that Cherubims had to be represented in human form. Furthermore,
in the temple, there were also blood and ashes of sacrificed animals; these
were then replaced by images of saints, since the rational took the place of
the irrational.[38] Here it is again a reminiscence of the Dionysian doctrine.
For him too, as described in *The Celestial Hierarchy*, one needs to go beyond simple appearances and to rightly interpret symbols. For Dionysius,
dissimilar symbols resist being immediately accepted and require an explanation. Once used to the idea of dissimilar symbols, the initiated can
proceed to the less surprising symbols, without understanding them literally. Then, the initiated has no more need of reminders regarding negations and dissimilarities, but simply incorporates this awareness into the
exegesis of symbols.[39] There is here a parallelism between the individual
and general plans—just as a beginner individual needs to get used to dissimilar symbols in order to proceed to similar ones, in the same manner,
all of humanity in, the beginning, needed the Old Testament's symbols
in order to proceed to images of the forthcoming epoch. Furthermore,
as there was a danger that the initiated could be misled in the literally
interpretation of dissimilar symbols, so there was a danger that the humanity of the times of the Old Testament would continue the idolatrous
practice—this was the purpose of the Old Testament's prohibitions.

36. *Oratio* III:26.

37. Nicephorus *Scripta* 769.

38. *Oratio* I:20.

39. Rorem, *Pseudo-Dionysius*, 57.

However, this danger does not exist anymore; the rational has replaced the irrational: "We are no longer enslaved by the elements of the law as children, but being restored to perfect manhood we are nourished with solid food, no longer prone to idolatry."[40]

The accusation of idolatry provoked a sensitive point of Christian belief—it posed the question whether images of Christ were acceptable since He is contemporaneously divine and human. The connection of the argument of idolatry with the Christological question becomes clear in John's argumentation. The prohibition of images and likeness was based on the absence of whatsoever "form in the day when the Lord spoke" in the Old Testament. However, together with the incarnation of the divine Logos in Jesus Christ, the situation has changed and the likeness with God was available.[41] Not every part of the Old Testament is automatically binding for the Church, which has now received "a more sacred and more divine legislation."[42] Before the incarnation in Christ, the representation of the Logos in an image would have been truly "inappropriate and alien."[43] The prohibition was addressed to those who lived before the epoch of grace and who had to be guided towards the recognition of the divine "monarchy," i.e., towards monotheism. All this was reversed—it is not the use, but the prohibition, of icons that now should be "inappropriate and alien." Because of this reversion, the iconoclasm is, for John, a "kind of docetism, an irreverence for the mystery of God-man." The reality of the incarnation provided the authorization for Christians to make icons.[44] To negate this means to diminish the genuineness of Christ's humanity, because "man has no characteristic more fundamental than this, to be represented in an image; what cannot be represented in this way is not a human being, but a failure."[45]

All the time after the birth of Christ was *sub specie incarnationis*, and just as Christ appeared to his disciples with all the attributes of humanity and was perceived with the eyes of faith, in the same manner he is also discernible now. The Verb became flesh, and after that, it did not become

40. *Oratio* I:21.

41. *Oratio* III:7.

42. Nicephorus *Scripta* 456.

43. Theodorus *Refutatio* 457.

44. *Oratio* II:16.

45. Theodorus *Refutatio* 444–45.

non-flesh. If God thought that the intellectual contemplation was sufficient, then He would have manifested Himself in a manner appropriate
to that. The question of the persistence of the incarnation was considered
in the context of the appropriate veneration, veneration "in spirit and in
truth." If God revealed Himself in flesh, in material form, then the veneration through material objects is also permissible. The act of God is one of
the central themes of Damascene's doctrine:

> The second kind of veneration is that whereby we venerate crea-
> tures, through whom and in whom God worked our salvation,
> either before the coming of the Lord, or in his incarnate dispensa-
> tion, such as Mount Sinai and Nazareth, the manger of Bethlehem
> and the cave, the holy place of Golgotha, the wood of the cross, the
> nails, the sponge, the reed, the holy and saving lance, the apparel,
> the tunic, the linen cloths, the winding sheet, the holy tomb, the
> fountain head of our resurrection, the gravestone, Sion the holy
> Mount, and again the Mount of Olives, the sheep gate and the
> blessed precinct of Gethsemane. These and suchlike I reverence
> and venerate and every holy temple of God and every place in
> which God is named, not because of their nature, but because they
> are receptacles of divine energy and in them God was pleased to
> work our salvation. And I reverence angels and human beings and
> all matter participating in divine energy and serving my salvation,
> and I venerate them because of the divine energy.[46]

The main feature of this argument is that the iconoclasts could not
manage to understand the way in which God had decided to operate—
God decided to manifest Himself through material objects and it is
through these objects that we venerate God. The argument is not limited
only to icons, but affirms that the sacred could be found everywhere, as
demonstrated by God, who chose such a vast variety of things to operate both His manifestation and our salvation.[47] Again, one can sense the
twofold movement, characteristic of Dionysius, of theophany and ascent
of man to God.

The material object and the contemplative mind are actively related
one to another, each helping the other to proceed towards further points
in the scale of being. As Theodore the Studite writes:

46. *Oratio* III:34.

47. See Henry, "What Was the Iconoclastic Controversy About?" 25–26.

> God is venerated in spirit and in truth, in an image, in the Book of
> Gospels, in the Cross and in every other consecrated thing, since
> material objects are uplifted through the mental elevation towards
> God. The mind does not stop at them . . . On the contrary, as the
> orthodox faith teaches, through them, it reaches the prototype.[48]

The veneration of icons is a process, not a procedure. And the material object participates in the divinity through grace—God chose to come
to humanity through matter.

The importance of material objects, i.e., symbols, through which
God manifested Himself, is reaffirmed in one of his letters: "If we accept the premise [of the iconoclasts], then vain is the image of the cross,
vain the form of the lance, vain the form of the sponge . . . and, to speak
Διονυσαϊκῶς, vain any other sensible images."[49] One of the notions
that helped Theodore to affirm the importance of visual perception is
φαντασία. In his letter to Naukratios he states that the soul possesses five
faculties—φαντασία, αἴσθησις, δόξα, διάνοια, νοῦς—the last four depend
upon φαντασία and for this reason, he defends the use of icons.[50] In the
*Parva Catechesis* Theodore affirms that the soul possesses only three faculties, and it seems likely that he put together φαντασία-αἴσθησις and
δόξα-διάνοια and saw them culminating in νοῦς; imagination and sense
perception leading to judgment, judgment leading to the final act of mind.
Here φαντασία becomes the part of αἴσθησις by which a pictorial image
is reflected and in which it remains stored—imagination as the source
of memory.[51] Similarly, for Damascene they are either essentially one or
are two parts of a single power. This line of thought contributed to the
understanding of sight as primary to other senses. It functioned through
the presence of light; its objects were colors, and the forms were perceived
by their color differentiations. Damascene wrote: "The first sense is sight
and the organs of sight are the nerves of the brain and the eyes." It was
natural for the iconodules to accept the primacy of sight over hearing and
other senses. It is in a somewhat different tone that the Areopagite will say,
speaking of our inability to be directly raised to conceptual contemplations, "We need our own upliftings that come naturally to us and which

48. Theodorus *Antirrheticus* 344D.

49. Theodorus *Epistolae* 1220B.

50. Ibid.

51. Mathew, *Byzantine Aesthetics*, 118.

can raise before us the permitted forms of the marvelous and unformed sights."[52] Or in a similar manner, "We now grasp these things in the best way we can, and as they come to us, wrapped in the sacred veils of that love toward humanity with which scripture and hierarchical traditions cover the truths of the mind with things derived from the realm of the senses."[53] And speaking of passing form senses to higher levels, "The truth we have to understand is that we use letters, syllables, phrases, written terms and words because of the senses. But when our souls are moved by intelligent energies in the direction of the things of the intellect then our senses and all that go with them are no longer needed."[54]

This sensitivity of veneration, as a complex human activity, represents the way in which man in the world establishes a relation with the world and with God who created both world and man. However, veneration is not the only human activity involved in the debate on images—the argument considers also the faculty to name things, and does not concern only named things. The question is if it is the icon itself that should be venerated or the name that it contains. The answer of Theodore claims that "the name is the name of the named thing, and could be considered as a kind of natural image of thing to which it refers, and, therefore, between the thing and its name there is no division of one and only veneration."[55] The argument establishes that names are not intellectual constructions; they are not arbitrary, but they represent one of the ways in which objects are made knowable to human beings. The intelligibility is given with the world—man's task is to recognize it, not to construct it. This aspect of Theodore's thought is fundamentally Platonic. As other iconodules, Theodore believed that the world makes itself accessible to man.[56]

The icon exemplifies a paradoxical vision that amalgamates similarity and dissimilarity. This vision has its origins in the Platonic and Neoplatonic traditions. Dionysius himself gave a rather Platonic exposition of the doctrine according to which God is similar to Himself and to nothing else, but, on the other hand, He gives the biggest possibility of similarity with Him to those who convert to Him. Dionysius writes,

52. Dionysius *De coelesti hierarchia* 140A.

53. Dionysius *De divinis nominibus* 592B.

54. Dionysius *De divinis nominibus* 708D.

55. Theodorus *Antirrheticus* 344D–345A.

56. See Henry, "What Was the Iconoclastic Controversy About?" 27.

"Things on the same level may be similar to one another with the result that similarity can be predicated of either of them. And they can be similar to each other through the workings of a prior form of similarity which they share. But an interchange of this sort cannot be admitted in regard to Cause and effects."[57] In other words, we should try to become similar to God, but God will not be similar to us.[58] Important here is another passage from Dionysius, found in *The Ecclesiastical Hierarchy*, which is quoted by Theodore[59]:

> In the domain of perceptible images, the artist keeps an eye constantly on the original and never allows himself to be sidetracked or to have his attention divided by any other visible object. If he does this, then one may presume to say that whatever the object which he wishes to depict he will, so to speak, produce a second one, so that one entity can be taken for the other, though in essence they are actually different.[60]

Obviously, this passage allowed the iconodules to reinforce their assertion that the image of Christ in a work of art can be identical to him in a way, but not in another: identical to the form of his humanity and with his divine-human hypostasis, but not identical to his invisible divine nature.

## THE COUNCIL OF NICAEA

The Seventh Ecumenical Council, the Second Council of Nicaea, held in 787, is the last universal council, recognized by both the Roman-Catholic and Orthodox Church. The Council restored definitely, in the theological and ecclesiastical sense, the veneration of icons. The acts of the Council contain main theses of the iconoclast party and their confutation by the Fathers.

In the first session, the participants of the Council accepted the doctrine of images expressed by the Roman Pope, and posed the question regarding the state of bishops who in 754 participated at the iconoclastic

---

57. Dionysius *De divinis nominibus* 913C–D.

58. See Ladner, "The Concept of the Image," 13.

59. Theodorus *Antirrheticus II* 357B.

60. Dionysius *De ecclesiastica hierarchia* 473C.

council of Hiereia. This question was resolved with a positive outcome at the third session, by allowing the bishops in question to attend the proceedings of the Council.

The last session proclaimed the official definition of the doctrine on images, accepted by all:

> ... as proceeding in the royal road and following the sacred doctrines of our holy fathers and the tradition of the Catholic Church, for this we acknowledge to be from the Divine Spirit that dwelleth in her, we with all exactness and care do define that, in the same manner as the Holy and Life giving Cross, so shall holy images, whether formed of colours or of stones, or any other convenient material, be set forth in all the holy churches of God, and also on sacred vessels and garments, on walls and doors, in houses and by the highways, whether images of Christ Jesus our Lord, our God and Saviour, or of our spotless Lady, the Holy Mother of God, or of the Holy Angels or of all the Saints and other holy men. For in proportion as these are continually seen by representation in images, so are they who behold them moved to the remembrance of, and affection for, their prototypes.
>
> And, further, we define that there be paid to them the worship of salutation and honour, and not that true worship which is according to faith, and which is due to the Divine Nature alone, but such worship as is properly paid to the image of the Holy and Life giving Cross and to the Holy Gospels, and to the other sacred monuments, and that the offering of incense and lights should be made to the honour of such things as was the pious custom of the ancients. For the honour of the image passes on to the prototype, and those who venerate an image venerate in it the person of him who is represented thereby. Thus is confirmed the doctrine of the holy fathers, thus the tradition of the Church which from end to end of the earth hath received the Gospel. Thus we follow Paul, speaking in Christ, and the whole company of Apostles and Fathers, holding fast the traditions which we have received. Thus we write in the hymns which spake in prophecy of the Church— "Rejoice greatly, O daughter of Zion: shout, O daughter of Israel: be glad and rejoice with all thine hearth. The Lord hath taken away [the wickedness of thine enemies]: He hath redeemed thee from the hand of thine adversaries. The Lord thy King is in the midst of thee: thou shalt not see evil any more, and peace shall be upon thee for ever."

> Those who dare to think or teach otherwise, or after the
> manner of accused Heretics to reject ecclesiastical tradition, or to
> imagine any innovations, or to cast out any of those things which
> have been brought into the Church—whether it be the Gospel, the
> type of the cross, or any picture, or any relic of a Martyr; or to
> reason perversely or craftily for the subversion of any of the legiti-
> mate traditions of the Church, or to use any of the precious things
> or of the sacred monasteries as profane things: if they be Bishops
> or Clergy let them be deposed; or if Monks or Laics let them be
> separated from communion.[61]

The Council affirmed that icons were part of the tradition of the Church,
which has received this tradition and feels called up to keep it alive.
Tradition is here the living bond connecting all generations of believers
with the historical origin of their Faith, and keeping this origin constantly
present. Therefore, the iconoclasts, who saw themselves as the restorers of
old tradition, would in fact reject the living tradition of which they themselves are part, which would mean that the living tradition loses its character of being a medium, which opens the truth to each generation.[62]

Further, the decision of the Council was based on the theological and
anthropological truth of the creation of man "in the image" of God—in
man God depicted Himself, and in Christ, by incarnation, God became
man, and, therefore, in the Church, as in an eternal and immortal community, the image and the prototype of the image are united. In the root
of the dogmatic decision made by the Council stands the Christological
dogma of the incarnation of God the Logos, God-man Jesus Christ, while
the image of the cross served as an exemplar of icons. Furthermore, the
decision accentuated the moral sense of the cult, and did not differentiate
between the cross and images of Christ and saints.[63]

The Council put the icons on the same level as the cross or other sacred objects. Those together form one unity, the harmonious decoration
of God's house. Those who reject or destroy the icons will soon abandon
the reverence of other sacred objects as well. On the other hand, the ven-

61. Mansi XIII:379–80.

62. Schönborn, *God's Human Face*, 203.

63. Tensek, "Teologija slike," 1071–72.

eration of the icons is part of that reverence due in general to all sacred objects.[64]

The acts of the Council make two explicit references to Dionysius the Areopagite. When, at the sixth session, the definition of the iconoclast council was read, followed by a confutation, John the deacon said, "Oh, would that, as they have in their commencement made use of the paternal voice of the hierophant Dionysius, they had preserved inviolate those traditions which he in common with the rest of the holy fathers held."[65] However, despite the declaration of John, it is not possible to identify the exact passage of the *Corpus Areopagiticum* the *Horos* quoted.

The second quotation of Dionysius refers to a passage from *The Divine Names*:

> Well would it have been for them had they been acquainted with the words of the God-fearing Dionysius as found in his discourse on the Hierarchy—"The resemblance of effects to their causes is not absolutely complete; for though the effects have an impress corresponding to their causes, yet the causes themselves are superior to the effects caused by them, and they are more important in proportion to the ratio of their own original."[66]

Besides these direct citations of Dionysius, one can feel an implicit presence of the Areopagite in the definition of the Council. For example, in claiming that more icons are being looked at, more are the ones who

64. Schönborn, *God's Human Face*, 205.

65. Mansi XIII:212A.

66. Mansi XIII:253E. Although the *Refutatio* mentions that the passages comes from the *Hierarchies*, it is in fact from *The Divine Names* (Dionysius *De divinis nominibus* 645C). Another passage seems to be a paraphrase that expresses the same idea: "Now while God is called 'same' to indicate that he is totally, uniquely, and undividedly like himself, he is also described as 'similar' and this is a divine name which we must not reject. The theologians say that the transcendent God is inherently similar to no other being, but that he also bestows a similarity to himself on all those who are returning to him in imitation as far as possible, of what is beyond all definition and understanding. It is the power of the divine similarity which returns all created things toward their Cause, and these things must be reckoned to be similar to God by reason of the divine image and likeness. But we cannot say that God is similar to them, any more than we can say that man is similar to his own portrait. Things on the same level may be similar to one another with the result that similarity can be predicated of either of them. And they can be similar to each other through the workings of a prior form of similarity which they share. But an interchange of this sort cannot be admitted in regard to Cause and effects, for God does not grant similarity merely to some objects." ( *De divinis nominibus* 913C–D.)

look at them uplifted to the memory and desire of prototypes, Fathers of the Council follow Dionysius' path and the pedagogical and anagogical purpose that he ascribes to symbols. Icon is nothing but an image that represents a likeness of the Prototype, and this is why the icon is venerable and saintly.[67] At the same time, the veneration is directed to the invisible and to the represented[68], and it is this miracle that orients the anagogical movement—icon is a sacramental symbol and transmits the presence of the divine-human totality. In this sense, the quality of the icon perfectly connects to the symbolic theology of the Areopagite. In this way, the Dionysian doctrine, both through direct citations and through the influence exerted on the defenders of icons, becomes incorporated in the definition of the Council, and, therefore, makes part of the theology of icon and also of the canon law of the Church.

## APOPHATICISM AND ICON

In the tradition of the Byzantine spirituality, and later of the Orthodox Church, there is an apparent contradiction between visible and invisible. The Orthodoxy, mystically abstinent to extreme, is most refractory to every imagination, to every visual or auditive representation, and to every "illusion" that would be an attempt to circumscribe the divinity in figures and forms. The ascetic research for the "impassive passion" purifies mystical life and rejects every φαντασία,[69] apparition, and visual or sensitive phenomenon.[70] However, on the other hand, it was the Orthodoxy that created the cult of icons and constructed the visible dimension of the Church by surrounding itself with images and symbols.

Often complementary to the apophaticism is the concept of deification (θέωσις). So, in Dionysius the Areopagite, it is stated:

> Since the union of divinized minds with the Light beyond all deity occurs in the cessation of all intelligent activity, the godlike unified minds who imitate these angels as far as possible praise it most appropriately through the denial of all beings. Truly and

67. Mansi XIII:344.

68. Mansi XIII:244B.

69. Although, for example, Theodore the Studite defended the importance of imagination (see nn. 50–51 above).

70. Evdokimov, *Teologia della bellezza*, 222.

> supernaturally enlightened after this blessed union, they discover
> that although it is the cause of everything, it is not a thing since it
> transcends all things in a manner beyond being.[71]

On the one hand, the light of which Dionysius speaks surpasses every description (apophaticism), and on the other, those who seek it participate in it to a certain extent (deification). This idea will be adopted by Gregory Palamas who will speak about apophaticism regarding the divine essence and deification regarding divine energies. These two doctrines represent pillars of Byzantine mysticism and are found in many theology contexts, such as the defense of images.

Both apophaticism and deification belong to the ambit of the so-called "unwritten tradition" of Byzantine Christianity. They cannot be found in the Scriptures, in canon law, or in the apostolic tradition. For Maximus the Confessor, for example, deification is a mystery of the Christian faith—the "theological mystagogy" is something that surpasses usual principles of authority. Salvation and deification are to be considered through the liturgical experience.[72] The apophatic language is fundamentally one of the aspects of the Greek grammar and consists of adding as prefix the privative alpha in order to negate a word. This method is in the first place applied to God. In his first *Oration*, John Damascene says:

> I believe in one God, the one beginning of all things, himself without beginning, uncreated, imperishable and immortal, eternal and everlasting, incomprehensible, bodiless, invisible, uncircumscribed, without form, one being beyond being, divinity beyond divinity . . .[73]

The words that John uses (ἄναρχον, ἄκτιστον, ἀθάνατον, ἀνώλεθρον, αἰώιον, ἀίδιον, ἀσώματον, ἀκατάληπτον, ἀόρατον, ἀπερίγραπτον, ἀσχημάτιστον) are all attributes that contain the privative alpha. In contrast to these negative attributes, John also speaks of the positive attributes of God, such as "being," "light," "substance," etc. However, he concludes that the best names are those that combine these two ways, such as "superessential essence." Furthermore, Damascene explains the difference between the Old and New Testaments' representations

---

71. Dionysius *De divinis nominibus* 593B–C.

72. Evdokimov, *Teologia della bellezza*, 223.

73. *Oratio* I:4.

of God by appealing to apophatic tradition. As a matter of fact, in the Old Testament, God is encountered in symbolic terms, while in the New Testament, this encounter occurs in image, in iconic form. Respecting the apophatic principles of Orthodox theology, his argument is that symbolic representations of God in the Old Testament are not God as such, since symbols expressed a negative statement about God in symbols which He cannot be. The symbol was a device by which God's affirmation might be approached through negation. On the other hand, the New Testament encounters God in an iconic manner, and while symbol speaks of God referentially, the icon touches on the reality of God, thus bringing one to the participation in the reality that the icon represents.[74]

Both ways, apophatic and cataphatic, are admissible, and should be used together. However, since the human language is not capable of comprehending the divinity, apophaticism would be more adequate, even though the knowledge of God could be on the other side of both apophaticism and cataphaticism.

Regarding the relation of the apophaticism to the iconological question, one could say that iconoclasm itself expresses in a certain sense the apophatic method. Meyendorff notes the belief in the absolute transcendence and invisibility of God was part of the Islamic anti-Christian polemics, and that the iconoclast emperors decided to "clean" the Church of idolatry in order to better combat against Islam; if this was true, then the apophaticism could have contributed to the development of iconoclasm.[75] However, as shown by the example of Dionysius, the apophaticism was already a stable doctrine in the Byzantine tradition, and, therefore, emperors would not have needed to refer to apophaticism coming from Islamic theology.[76]

Theodore the Studite also used apophatic language in his writings. For him, it is clear to everyone that the divinity is incomprehensible, uncircumscribed, without limits, and without form, and should be attributed with the names that signify denial. According to the theological doctrine, away from any kind of circumscription or comprehension, we do not know even if God exists, nor what characteristics He has.[77] The

74. Hieromonk Auxentios, "The Iconic and Symbolic in Orthodox Iconography."

75. Meyendorff, *The Byzantine Legacy in the Orthodox Church*, 23.

76. Parry, *Depicting the Word*, 117–18.

77. Theodorus *Antirrheticus* 329C–D.

nature of the divinity is such that it remains on the other side of every predication.

On the other hand, the deification is operated through Christ and represents the restoration of the relationship that man originally had with God. Since human beings are not capable of comprehending the divinity individually, deification can succeed only through grace. The Byzantine vision of grace has its origins precisely in the writings of the Areopagite. Grace is viewed as cooperation between God and man, since man cannot depend only on grace, nor can he rely only on his own capacities. Deification is seen as a process, not as an event—it is the present possibility and future hope, based on the restoration of the capacity to receive grace, operated through Jesus Christ. Such vision found its place in the words of the Fathers of the Council of Nicaea:

> God, therefore, and the Word of the Father, who became without change of nature perfect Man, having recovered him from the fall and delivered him from the errors of idolatry, reconstructed him for immortality, and bestowed on him the gift which is without repentance. This gift was more God-like than the forms, the reconstruction exceeded the original formation, and the benefit is eternal.[78]

Man, however, is not being deified by nature, but by adoption. Even though he is created in the image of God, man is subjected to death and in this, he shares the destiny of earthly animals. Saints too are described as "the likeness of God," and they are called gods not by nature, but by adoption. The role of this negation "not by nature" was, as we have seen, very much used by the iconodules. In fact, the distinction between nature and adoption is the distinction between creator and creation. Only God is divine by nature. In addition, Nicephorus makes this distinction by distinguishing the relation of man to God by adoption and grace (θέσις καὶ χάρις) from the relation of the Son to the Father by nature and potency (φύσις καὶ δύναμις).[79]

Incarnation is the analogy for human deification. Deification of human nature is not an absorption in the divinity. On the contrary, as the

---

78. Mansi XIII:216A.

79. Nicephorus *Scripta* 421D–424A.

iconodules underlined, even after his ascension to heaven, Christ maintains his human nature.

Deification highlights the importance of the entire person, endowed with both soul and body, and this is the reason why Christ took both human elements in order to become man in his fullness. Therefore, the entire man becomes deified, and here we find a theological anthropology that affirms the fullness of man—this anthropology will mark the path of the entire Byzantine and Orthodox spirituality.

For Theodore the Studite, the divinity is present everywhere, in rational and irrational beings, animate and inanimate. However, the measure of the presence of the divinity depends on the nature that receives it. Therefore, it would not be a mistake to say that the divinity is found even in icon, and in the same way, in the cross and in other sacred objects. Howbeit, the divinity is not present in them according to the union of natures, since they are not deified flesh, but according to relative participation.[80] On the other hand, it would be wrong by venerating icon to venerate Christ's divinity, as if it were naturally present in the icon.[81] The difference stands in the distinction between theology and economy—the veneration in spirit and in truth belongs to theology, while the veneration of Christ in image belongs to economy.[82]

The apophaticism of the divinity is moderated by the grace of the economy. The paradox that God is not like us, but we are like Him, presents our relationship with God, which is at the same time close and distant. We cannot comprehend the divine transcendence, but we can sense something of its presence.[83]

An icon "sanctifies the eyes of those who see and uplifts intelligence to the level of God-knowing" in a mystical way. Above the discourse, there is the divine illumination, the invisible, the inaudible, and the ineffable. The contemplation, at its end, is of intuitive kind, ineffable and transdiscursive. According to the word of Dionysius:

> ["Light of the mind"] renews all the powers of their minds. It steps beyond everything inasmuch as it is ordered beyond everything. It

80. Theodorus *Antirrheticus* 344C.

81. Theodorus *Antirrheticus* 349D.

82. Theodorus *Antirrheticus* III 428B.

83. Parry, *Depicting the Word*, 123–24.

precedes everything inasmuch as it transcends everything. Quite simply, it gathers together and supremely anticipates in itself the authority of all illuminating power, being indeed the source of light and actually transcending light. And so it assembles into a union everything possessed of reason and of mind.[84]

The icon is a symbolic-hypostatic representation that invites the viewer to transcend the symbol, to communicate to the hypostasis, in order to participate in the indescribable. It is a way through which one should pass in order to surpass it. This does not mean to abolish it, but to discover its transcendent dimension.[85] The icon meets the Hypostasis and introduces itself into the experience of the naked presence of empirical forms:

> The icon does not lead towards the pure and simple absence of image, but, above and on the other side of image, towards the indescribable Hyper-icon, and this is its apophatic aspect, the iconographic apophaticism. The icon is the last arrow of human eros sent to the heart of the Mystery.[86]

In this manner, the notions of apophaticism and deification, together with the doctrine of icon, remind one of the thought of Dionysius the Areopagite. His doctrine of God's transcendence and immanence reflects the apophatic theology and deification—while it is not possible to say anything about God who is incomprehensible and invisible, it is possible to feel His presence in the world, through sensible object through which He Himself has chosen to manifest Himself to humanity. As Jean-Luc Marion has nicely said on distinguishing the idol and the icon:

> In the idol, the reflex of the mirror distinguishes the visible from that which exceeds the aim . . . in the icon, the visible is deepened infinitely in order to accompany, as one may say, each point of the invisible by a point of light. But visible and invisible thus coexist to infinity . . . The invisible of the icon consists of the intention of the face. The more the face becomes visible, the more the invisible intention whose gaze envisages us becomes visible. Better: the visibility of the face allows the invisibility that envisages to grow.[87]

84. Dionysius *De divinis nominibus* 701A–B.

85. Evdokimov, *Teologia della bellezza*, 226.

86. Ibid.

87. Marion, *God Without Being*, 20.

# Conclusion

The symbolic theory of Dionysius the Areopagite provided a decisive weapon to the defenders of the holy images. The concept of icon as anagogical instrument and books for the illiterate, the manifestation of God through material objects, the essential importance of symbols in the religious life, the relation image-prototype, the apophatic and deifying sense of icon—those are all notions derived from Dionysius, which were skilfully used by iconodules for the definition of their doctrine. The Dionysian influence on John Damascene and Theodore the Studite is evident. But beyond the definitive victory of icons in the Christian tradition, the Areopagite and the main exponents of iconolatrous doctrine contributed to the development of two other phenomena, of more general significance, on which I would like to focus our attention.

The first is the formation of the Byzantine aesthetics. As all the other products of Byzantine spirit, the aesthetics was formed on two main pillars—the inheritance of the ancient Greece and the revelation of the Christian faith. Byzantine masters synthesized these two worlds, which have also marked future epochs of European history. The Byzantine aesthetics was preoccupied with transcendent beauty. As Byzantines thought, man lived on earth, but heaven was his true homeland. In accordance with this attitude, the scope of human activities, comprising art, was to prepare man for his return back to his homeland. Works of art were not conceived as goals to themselves, but were considered instruments, intermediaries between heaven and earth, between God and man. This may be why the Byzantine aesthetics does not contain artistic poetics, but the canon of art was established and defined in a speculative manner, by thinkers, theologians, and philosophers. This was a consequence of the exaltation of the transcendence of the world in Byzantine culture.

On the other hand, Byzantine art was conceived in a grandiose manner, after the parallelism with the imperial court. In Byzantine churches, all arts had to collaborate in order to realize this goal—images and mosaics, monumental architecture, beauty of liturgical vestments, symphony of chant and word in the liturgy, had to provoke an aesthetic sentiment, and this aesthetic sentiment uplifted the soul to God. This is why the Byzantine ritual was characterized by the so-called "material mysticism." The material splendor was used to circulate mystical ideas and represented a way to God through the aesthetic experience. The pleasure of sights and sounds represented promises of celestial bliss.[1] The heavenly order, the order of the true world, was mirrored in the ceremonies of the court and in ecclesiastical services. Solemnity and splendor were essential elements in connecting men with the heavenly order. In the eyes of Byzantines, these were not just varieties of luxuries but genuine images of the divine world. God was expressed in the imperial and ecclesiastical magnificence and order, which were universally regarded as divine and holy.[2]

The mystical thought of Dionysius the Areopagite played an important role in the formation of such conception of art, but there was, however, the influence of that Greek inheritance in the sense of the need for beauty and grandiose ceremony:

> The Greeks believed only in what they could see and touch. Thus it was in the time of Phidias and thus it was to remain during the Byzantine period. But the object of belief underwent a radical change. In ancient Greece, it was a pantheistic deity; in medieval Byzantium, a transcendent God, embodying the idea of the purest spirituality.[3]

All the sensible and material splendor was moderated by the mysticism and symbolism in Byzantine art which proceeded from spiritual and transcendent aesthetics. In the words of Dionysius:

> A hierarchy has God as its leader of all understanding and action. It is forever looking directly at the comeliness of God. A hierarchy bears in itself the mark of God. Hierarchy causes its members to be images of God in all respects, to be clear and spotless mirrors

1. Tatarkiewicz, *Medieval Aesthetics*, 36.
2. Kazhdan and Constable, *People and Power*, 158.
3. Lazarev, *Istoriya vizantijskoj zhivopisi*, 27.

reflecting the glow of primordial light and indeed of God himself. It ensures that when its members have received this full and divine splendor they can then pass on this light generously and in accordance with God's will to beings further down the scale.[4]

In the iconic representations, especially after the time of iconoclasm, gold has a particular significance. The golden color represents the light, which has not a purpose to create illusions, but irradiates from icon itself towards the spectator. The bodies represented on icons do not receive the light from outside, but bear their own light, which springs from their inside. The light reflects eternal ideas that are in the basis of these bodies. It transposes divine energies, of which the uncreated Tabor is a vision, which supports distinct beings and takes them to deification.[5] Obviously, the iconic significance of light derives directly from Dionysius, who gave the most complete theory of light in relation to God, beauty and the beautiful. According to him, the light, which is an ontological-gnoseological category, is primarily connected to the "good," which is a vivifying quality of the divinity, and through which everything receives its state of existence.[6] This notion of light concerns both visible light, which is perceptible with senses, and the spiritual light. In this way, the good communicates the splendor of this light to all rational substances:

> The Good is described as the light of the mind because it illuminates the mind of every supra celestial being with the light of the mind, and because it drives from souls the ignorance and the error squatting there. It gives them all a share of sacred light. It clears away the fog of ignorance from the eyes of the mind and it stirs and unwraps those covered over by the burden of darkness. At first it deals out the light in small amounts and then, as the wish and the longing for light begin to grow, it gives more and more of itself, shining ever more abundantly on them because they "loved much", and always it keeps urging them onward and upward as their capacity permits.[7]

All the information in the structure of the celestial hierarchy and from celestial to terrestrial levels is transmitted in the form of the spiritual

4. Dionysius *De coelesti hierarchia* 165A.

5. Besançon, *The Forbidden Image*, 136.

6. Dionysius *De divinis nominibus* 696D.

7. Dionysius *De divinis nominibus* 700D–701A.

light, which assumes the countenance of the visible splendor. The luminous information (or, "the gift of light") is the principle mediator between the transcendent and immanent levels of being, and is mysteriously concealed under "sacred veils," such as images, sensible representations and symbols organized in conformity to the possibility of our perception. In this way, the spiritual light, which is not accessible to human perception, constitutes however the main content of material images, symbols, etc., phenomena created expressly for its transmission, including the images of oratory and figurative art.[8]

From the doctrine of icons established by great iconophile theologians arose an unusual theory of art in the history of aesthetics: image was understood as a fragment of the divinity, and was judged according to its likeness with the prototype. Never again, in the history of aesthetics, was such a radical theory of art been proposed.[9] Thanks to the iconophile theory, works of art acquired a mystical value, a phenomenon that never happened in the West.

Icons were not destined only to be looked upon, but were made for prayer in long and concentrated contemplation, in order to bring the mind towards the contemplation of God—image was, therefore, an instrument, not a goal.

This entire conception of art was possible thanks to some fundamental points of the Byzantine vision of the world. There are two worlds, earthly and heavenly, material and spiritual. The spiritual world is of principal importance, as it contains the archetypes according to which the material world is made. Although he lives in the earthly world, as already said, man's true destination is not earth, but heaven; however, this material world is not completely evil, since God descended and dwelt in it.

The second phenomenon whose importance I would like to underline is closely connected to the non-evilness of the earthly world—the body. The entire iconoclastic controversy, in doctrinal sense, could be reduced to the dualism between material and spiritual, body and soul. From the iconoclasts' position, one can deduce that for them the only thing worthy of veneration was the divinity, i. e., the divine aspect of Christ, immaterial and incorporeal. Obviously, they despised matter and

8. Bychkov, *L'estetica bizantina*, 114–15.

9. Tatarkiewicz, *Medieval Aesthetics*, 42.

considered it unworthy and evil. On the other hand, the defense of the possibility of representing Christ and saints in human form, made by the iconodules, implied that for them matter should not be rejected or underestimated—the fact that God Himself manifested through matter means that it should be respected.

Symbols used in the liturgy, symbolic figures in the Scriptures, images of Christ and saints represented human form, belong to the material world and open the door to a celestial world, immaterial and spiritual. Therefore, the body, also made of matter, finds its place in the Christian-Byzantine anthropological doctrine. The conception of the body as the "prison" of the soul[10] had no success in Byzantine religious thought. As John Damascene writes:

> I do not venerate matter, I venerate the fashioner of matter, who became matter for my sake and accepted to dwell in matter and through matter worked my salvation, and I will not cease from reverencing matter, through which my salvation was worked.[11]

With his symbolic doctrine, Dionysius the Areopagite was the source of the positive consideration of matter. Spiritual things are manifested through material things, and every material thing participates in a certain grade, as a fragment of the divinity, in the spiritual world. Man himself was made to the image of God, and he is constituted of both soul and body. To negate matter, i. e., body, would mean to negate the fullness of man and to underestimate the work of God. Speaking of icons, Theodore the Studite will say:

> Should somebody say "Since I ought to venerate [Christ] in spirit, it is pointless to venerate him in his icon," he should know that with this he also abandons the spiritual veneration of Christ. You see, if he, in his spiritual contemplation, does not behold Christ in human form at the right hand of the Father, then he does not venerate him at all. On the contrary, he denies that the Word has

---

10. And this is exactly what implied the doctrine of the iconoclasts who argued that it was wrong to represent the human form of Christ—according to them, after the resurrection, Christ abandoned his human form, and what remains is his divinity which cannot be circumscribed.

11. *Oratio* I:16.

become flesh. But Christ's icon is a reliable testimony to the fact
that the Eternal Word has become one like us.[12]

Here we clearly see that the Christian icon is not identical to the
image in Platonic tradition: the icon does not refer to a purely spiritual
reality, but to the Lord who is risen in his body. True, the icon is imperfect, but not because it belongs to the material world, for Christ himself
belongs to it in his glorified body. Therefore, it would not be right to completely concentrate on the icon, nor it would be correct to attempt to gain
a completely spiritual contemplation without images. The icon veneration
is both visual and spiritual—in the visible likeness of Christ we venerate
his mystery spiritually.[13]

The consideration of material symbols as fragments of the divinity
finds an expression, precious also from an aesthetic point of view, in the
words of Dionysius:

> So, then, forms, even those drawn from the lowliest matter, can be
> used, not unfittingly, with regard to heavenly beings. Matter, after
> all, owes its subsistence to absolute beauty and keeps, throughout
> its earthly ranks, some echo of intelligible beauty. Using matter,
> one may be lifted up to the immaterial archetypes.[14]

The image, which reflects or designates the spiritual archetype,
is necessary to elevate man towards this inconceivable prototype. This
elevation, as we have seen in Dionysius' theories, is carried out with a
stimulus of the subject's psyche, through sensible images organized with
purpose. The image has to stimulate principally the subconscious sphere
of psyche and direct its activity to the channel of the individual spiritual
contemplation.[15]

Both Dionysius and iconodules understood this inseparable relation
of matter and spirit. They have not only elaborated the mystical theology
or defended the eminent place of icons, but bequeathed to future times a
conception of even more general significance—the goodness of the body.
This conception marked the entire history of Byzantine spirituality and
continued to live in the tradition of the Orthodox Church.

12. Theodorus *Epistolae* 1288C–D.

13. Schönborn, *God's Human Face*, 230.

14. Dionysius *De coelesti hierarchia* 144BC.

15. Bychkov, *L'estetica bizantina*, 167.

The though of Dionysius the Areopagite occupied an eminent place in Byzantine intellectual history. The contents of his works ensured that Dionysius maintained that place, albeit with uncertainties regarding his true identity. The mystical, but also aesthetic, character of his thought determined the course of Christian spirituality, especially in the Orient. From an aesthetic point of view, two main characteristics of his doctrine, the transcendence of the divinity and its immanence in the world, are analogous to the foundations of Byzantine art—through material and visible beauty the transcendent and invisible divinity is celebrated. André Guillou beautifully writes,

> Dés le début du Ve siécle, les images artistiques étaient mises par le Pseudo-Denys l'Aréopagite sur le même plan que les sacrements et l'oeuvre d'art à Byzance eut toujours une quintuple fonction: didactique, allégorique, mystique, liturgique et artistique; et l'on estime qu'elle éliminait chez le récepteur de l'image les antinomies de la pensée spéculative sur le dogme . . . Images, comme textes sacrés, sont aussi des symboles nés pour révéler et en même temps cacher la vérité, tels la liturgie, les sacrements, le culte en général. Elles sont de nécessaires intermédiaires pour s'élever jusqu'au spirituel et la clef pour en déchiffrer le code s'appelle la théologie, qui est la participation à Dieu, mais aussi compréhension du monde.[16]

The thought that the earthly world is an image of a better heavenly world is the most optimistic inheritance that can be given to man. And with such optimism I would like to conclude this work with the words of Dionysius:

*Καὶ οὐκ ἔ ϛτι τι τῶν ὄντων, ὅ μὴ μετέχει τοῦ καλοῦ καὶ ἀγαθοῦ*

---

16. André Guillou, "Prefazione," in Bychkov, *L'estetica bizantina*, 5–6.

# Bibliography

PRIMARY SOURCES
*(see also frequently cited works listed in Abbreviations)*

Dionysius Areopagita. *De coelesti hierarchia.* Columns 115–369 in PG 3.
———. *De divinis nominibus.* Columns 586–997 in PG 3.
———. *De ecclesiastica hierarchia.* Columns 369–586 in PG 3.
———. *Epistolae.* Columns 1065–1125 in PG 3.
———. *De mystica theologia.* Columns 997–1065 in PG 3.
———. *Tutte le opere.* Translated by Piero Scazzoso. Introduction, preface, paraphrase, notes, and index by Enzo Bellini. Milano: Rusconi, 1981.
Pseudo-Dionysius. *The Complete Works.* Translated by Colm Luibheid. Foreword, notes, and translation collaboration by Paul Rorem. Preface by René Roques. Introductions by Jaroslav Pelikan, Jean Leclercq and Karlfried Froehlich. New York: Paulist, 1987.
John of Damascus. *Difesa delle immagini sacre—Discorsi apologetici contro coloro che calunniano le sante immagini.* Translation, introduction, and notes by Vittorio Fazzo. Rome: Città Nuova Editrice, 1983.
———. *Three Treatises on the Divine Images.* Translation and introduction by Andrew Louth. St. Vladimir's Seminary Press Popular Patristics Series. New York: St. Vladimir's Seminary Press, 2003.
Nicephorus Constantinopolitanus. *Scripta adversus Iconomachos.* Columns 202–851 in PG 100.
*The Seventh General Council, the Second of Nicaea held A.D. 787, in which the Worship of Images was Established.* Translated by Rev. John Mendham. London: Painter, 1850.
Theodorus Studita. *Adversus Iconomachos Capita Septem.* Columns 486–98 in PG 99.
———. *Antirrheticus Primus adversus Iconomachos.* Columns 327–51 PG 99.
———. *Antirrheticus II.* Columns 351–90 in PG 99.
———. *Antirrheticus III.* Columns 390–435 in PG 99,
———. *Epistolae.* Columns 904–1670 in PG 99.
———. *Problemata ad Iconomachos.* Columns 478–86 in PG 99.
———. *Refutatio Poematum Iconomachorum.* Columns 435–78 in PG 99.
Theophanes. *Chronographia.* Ex recensione Ioannis Classeni. CSHB 1.
*Vedere l'invisibile—Nicea e lo statuto dell'Immagine.* Edited by Luigi Russo. Translated by Claudio Gerbino. Notes by Claudio Gerbino and Mario Re. Palermo: Aesthetica, 1997.

## SECONDARY LITERATURE

Auxentios (hieromonk). "The Iconic and Symbolic in Orthodox Iconography." A presentation given to a graduate seminar at the Graduate Theological Union, Berkeley, in the spring semester 1987.

Barasch, Moshe. *Icon: Studies in the History of an Idea.* New York: New York University Press, 1995.

Bergmann, Sigurd. *Creation Set Free: The Spirit as Liberator of Nature.* Sacra Doctrina. Grand Rapids: Eerdmans, 2005

Besançon, Alain. *The Forbidden Image: An Intellectual History of Iconoclasm.* Translated by Jane Marie Todd. Chicago: University of Chicago Press, 2000.

Bouyer, Louis. *Cosmos: The World and the Glory of God.* Translated by Pierre de Fontnouvelle. Petersham, MA: St. Bede's, 1988.

Brown, Peter. "A Dark-Age Crisis: Aspects of the Iconoclastic Controversy." *The English Historical Review* 346 (1973) 1–34.

Bychkov, Viktor. *L'estetica bizantina: Problemi teorici.* Idee, simboli, immagini / Università degli studi du Bari, Centro di studi Bizantini 1. Bari: Congedo, 1983.

Coakley, Sara, and Charles M. Stang, editors. *Rethinking Dionysius the Areopagite.* Directions in Modern Theology. Oxford: Wiley-Blackwell, 2009.

Corsini, Eugenio. *Il trattato 'De divinis nominibus' dello pseudo-Dionigi: e i commenti neoplatonici al Parmenide.* Torino: Giappichelli, 1962.

Evdokimov, Pavel. *Teologia della bellezza: L'arte dell'icona.* Rome: Paoline, 1984.

Florovsky, Georges. "Origen, Eusebius and the Iconoclastic Controversy." *Church History* 19 (1950) 77–96.

———. *Vizantiyskie Otcy V-VIII vekov.* Paris: YMCA Press, 1990.

Gambino, Rosanna. "L'icona di Cristo come ipostasi composta negli Antirretici di Teodoro Studita." In *Contrarietas: Saggi sui saperi medievali,* edited by Alessandro Musco, 31–56. Palermo: Officina di Studi Medievali, 2002.

Gero, Stephen. *Byzantine Iconoclasm During the Reign of Leo III, with Particular Attention to the Oriental Sources.* Corpus scriptorum Christianorum Orientalium 346. Leuven: Peeters, 1973

Gersh, Stephen. *From Iamblichus to Eriugena: An Investigation of the Prehistory and Evolution of the Pseudo-Dionysian Tradition.* Studien zur Problemgeschichte der antiken und mittelalterlichen Philosophie 8. Leiden: Brill, 1978.

Grabar, André. *L'iconoclasme byzantin: Dossier archéologique.* Paris: Collège de France, 1957.

Gregory, Timothy E. *A History of Byzantium.* Blackwell History of the Ancient World. Oxford: Blackwell, 2005.

Hathaway, Ronald F. *Hierarchy and the Definition of Order in the "Letters" of Pseudo-Dionysius. A Study in the Form and Meaning of the Pseudo-Dionysian Writings.* The Hague: Nijhoff, 1969.

Hausherr, Irénée. "Doutes au sujet du 'Divin Denys.'" *Orientalia Christiana Periodica* 2 (1936) 484–90.

Henry, Patrick. "What Was the Iconoclastic Controversy About?" *Church History* 45 (1976) 16–31.

Ivanovic, Filip. "Ancient EROS and Medieval AGAPE—the Concept of Love in Plato and Maximus the Confessor." In *Greek Philosophy and the Issues of Our Age II*, edited by K. Boudouris and M. Adam, 93–114. Athens: Ionia, 2009.

Kazhdan, Alexander, and Giles Constable. *People and Power in Byzantium: An Introduction to Modern Byzantine Studies.* Washington, DC: Dumbarton Oaks Center for Byzantine Studies, 1982.

Kharlamov, Vladimir. *The Beauty of the Unity and the Harmony of the Whole: The Concept of* Theosis *in the Theology of Pseudo-Dionysius the Areopagite.* Eugene, OR: Wipf & Stock, 2009.

Kitzinger, Ernst. "The Cult of Images in the Age before Iconoclasm." *Dumbarton Oaks Papers* 8 (1954) 83–150.

Koch, Hugo. *Die altchristliche Bilderfage nach den literarischen Quellen.* Göttingen: Vandenhoeck. & Ruprecht, 1917.

———. "Proklus als Quelle des Pseudo-Dionysius Areopagita in der Lehre von Bösen." *Philologus* 54 (1895) 438–54.

Ladner, Gerhard B. "The Concept of The Image in the Greek Fathers and the Byzantine Iconoclastic Controversy." *Dumbarton Oaks Papers* 7 (1954) 1–34.

———. *Images and Ideas in the Middle Ages: Selected Studies in History and Art.* Storia e Letteratura 155–56. Rome: Edizioni di storia e letteratura, 1983.

Lazarev, Viktor N. *Istoriya vizantijskoj zhivopisa.* Moscow: Iskusstvo, 1947.

Lilla, Salvatore. "Introduzione allo studio dello Ps. Dionigi l'Areopagita." *Augustinianum* 22.3 (1982) 533–77.

Lossky, Vladimir. *The Mystical Theology of the Eastern Church.* Crestwood, NY: St. Vladimir's Seminary Press, 1976.

Louth, Andrew. "St. Denys the Areopagite and the Iconoclast Controversy." In *Denys l'Aréopagite et sa postérité en orient et en occident*, edited by Ysabele de Andia, 329–39. Paris: Institut d'Études Augustiniennes, 1997.

———. *St. John Damascene: Tradition and Originality in Byzantine Theology.* Oxford Early Christian Studies. Oxford: Oxford University Press, 2002.

———. "'Truly Visible Things Are Manifest Images of Invisible Things': Dionysius the Areopagite on Knowing the Invisible." In *Seeing the Invisible in Late Antiquity and the Early Middle Ages*, edited by Giselle de Nie, Karl F. Morrison, and Marco Mostert, 15–24. Utrecht Studies in Medieval Literacy 14. Turnhout: Brepols, 2005.

Lowden, John. *Early Christian and Byzantine Art.* Art and Ideas. London: Phaidon, 2008.

Marion, Jean-Luc. *God Without Being: Hors-texte.* Religion and Postmodernism. Chicago: Chicago University Press, 1991.

Mathew, Gervase. *Byzantine Aesthetics.* New York: Harper & Row, 1971.

Mazzucchi, Carlo Maria. "Damascio, autore del *Corpus Dionysiacum*, e il dialogo Περὶ πολιτικῆς ἐπιστήμης." *Aevum* 80 (2006) 299–334.

Meyendorff, John. *The Byzantine Legacy in the Orthodox Church.* New York: St. Vladimir's Seminary Press, 1982.

———. *Byzantine Theology: Historical Trends and Doctrinal Themes.* New York: Fordham University Press, 1979.

Ostrogorsky, Georges. "Le début de la Querelle des Images." In *Mélanges Charles Diehl*, 1:235–55. Paris: Leroux, 1930.

———. *Istorija Vizantije.* Belgrade: BIGZ, 1998.

Ouspensky, Leonid. *Theology of the Icon*. 2 vols. Translated by Anthony Gythiel with selections translated by Elizabeth Meyendorff. Crestwood, NY: St. Vladimir's Seminary Press, 1992.

Parry, Kenneth. *Depicting the Word: Byzantine Iconophile Thought of the Eighth and Ninth Centuries*. The Medieval Mediterranean 12. Leiden: Brill, 1996.

Pelikan, Jaroslav. *The Spirit of Eastern Christendom (600–1700)*. The Christian Tradition: A Hisotry of the Development of Doctrine 2. Chicago: University of Chicago Press, 1974.

Radovic, Amfilohije. *Το μυστήριον της Αγίας Τριάδος κατά τον άγιον Γρηγόριον Παλαμάν*. Thessaloniki: PIPM, 1973

Riordan, William K. *Divine Light: The Theology of Denys the Areopagite*, San Francisco: Ignatius, 2008.

Rist, John. "Pseudo-Dionysius, Neoplatonism and the Weakness of the Soul." In: *From Athens to Chartres: Neoplatonism and Medieval Thought: Studies in Honour of Edouard Jeaneau*, edited by Haijo Jan Westra, 135–61. Studien und Texte zur Geistesgeschichte des Mittelalters 35. Leiden: Brill, 1992.

Rorem, Paul. *Biblical and Liturgical Symbols within the Pseudo-Dionysian Synthesis*. Studies and Texts 71. Toronto: Pontifical Institute of Mediaeval Studies, 1984.

———. *Pseudo-Dionysius: A Commentary on the Texts and an Introduction to Their Influence*. New York: Oxford University Press, 1993.

Roques, René. "Denys l'Aréopagite." In *Dictionnaire de spiritualité*, vol. 3. Paris: Beauchesne, 1957.

———. *L'univers dyonisien*. Paris: Aubier, 1954.

Saïd, Suzanne. "Images grecques: Icônes et idoles." *Faits de langues* 1.1 (1993) 11–20.

Schönborn, Christoph von. *God's Human Face: The Christ-Icon*. San Francisco: Ignatius, 1994.

Stiglmayr, Josef. "Der Neuplatoniker Proklos als Vorlage des sog. Dionysius Areopagita in der Lehre vom Übel." *Historisches Jahrbuch* 16 (1895) 253–73.

———. "Eine syrische Liturgie als Vorlage des Pseudo-Areopagite." *Zeitschrift für Katolische Theologie* 33 (1909) 383–85.

Strezova, Anita. "Relation of Image to its Prototype in Byzantine Iconophile Theology." *Byzantinoslavica* 66 (2008) 87–106.

Tatarkiewicz, Wladislaw. *Medieval Aesthetics. History of Aesthetics*, vol. 2. Edited by C. Barrett. Translated by Adam and Ann Czerniawski. London: Continuum, 2006.

Teníek, Tomislav Zdenko. "Teologija slike, s posebnim naglaskom na patrističko razdoblje", *Bogoslovska smotra* 74 (2004) 1043–78.

Vasiliev, Alexander. A. *History of the Byzantine Empire, 324–1453*. Vol. 1. Madison: University of Wisconsin Press, 1980

Zoubouli, Maria. "La Conception byzantine de l'art plastique." *Europe* 75 (1997) 115–20.

# Index